# Laughing Matters
## A Serious Look at Humour

'Punch Puppet', from Professor Hoffmann's, *Drawing Room Amusements*. (1879)

# Laughing Matters
# A Serious Look at Humour

*Edited by*

**JOHN DURANT** and **JONATHAN MILLER**

Copublished in the United States with
John Wiley & Sons, Inc., New York

**Longman Scientific & Technical**
Longman Group UK Limited
Longman House, Burnt Mill, Harlow
Essex CM20 2JE, England
*and Associated Companies throughout the world.*

Copublished in the United States with
John Wiley & Sons Inc., 605 Third Avenue, New York,
NY 10158

First published in 1988

**British Library Cataloguing in Publication Data**

Laughing matters – a serious look at humour.
1. Man. Humour – Sociological perspectives
I. Durant, John   II. Miller, Jonathan
302.5
ISBN 0-582-03162-1

**Library of Congress Cataloging in Publication Data available**

ISBN 0-470-21185-7  (Wiley)

Produced by Longman Group (FE) Limited
Printed in Hong Kong

# Contents

# Acknowledgements

This book is based on a programme of lectures given under the auspices of Section X (General) of the British Association for the Advancement of Science during the Annual Meeting of the Association which took place on 24–28 August 1987 at the Queen's University of Belfast. This lecture programme could not have been arranged without the help of many different people and agencies. The Belfast local organizing committee provided excellent facilities for the meeting; John Banfield, the Section X local secretary, took great pains to ensure that the programme ran smoothly, and Jasia Reichardt provided a marvellous synchronized tape – slide show during the meeting.

The work described in Chapter 2 was supported by NIH grants NS 11408 and 06029, the Research Service of the Veterans Administration, and Harvard Project Zero. Hiram Brownell and Howard Gardner would like to thank Nancy Lefkowitz and other personnel of the Spalding Rehabilitation Hospital for their help in this research, and Ray Molloy and Joan Ostrove for comments on earlier drafts of their chapter.

Section X of the British Association for the Advancement of Science is grateful to Unisys Ltd, who provided much-needed support for their Belfast programme. In particular, thanks are due to Tony Higgins, the Unisys press affairs manager, for his personal support for the work of Section X over many years. In addition, the Section is pleased to acknowledge the support of the Institute for Scientific Information, who once again kindly underwrote a number of its social functions in Belfast.

The Publishers would like to thank *The Sunday Telegraph* for permission to reproduce the cartoon by Garland on page 86, the *London Evening Standard* for Low's cartoon on page 82, and the *New Statesman* for Vicky's cartoon on page 84.

# About the editors

**John Durant** is the Recorder of Section X (General) of the British Association for the Advancement of Science. He is a zoologist and a historian of science, with special interests in evolutionary theory and the relationship between animal and human behaviour. His most recent publication (co-authored under the pseudonym John Klama) is *Aggression: Conflict in Animals and Humans Reconsidered*, which was published earlier this year by Longman Group (UK) and John Wiley (USA). He is currently Staff Tutor in Biological Sciences in the Department for External Studies, University of Oxford.

**Jonathan Miller** is a doctor of medicine and a film, theatre and opera director. Having qualified in medicine in 1959, he worked in hospitals for two years, and then co-authored and appeared in 'Beyond the Fringe'. As a director, he has undertaken a number of films for BBC television, including *Alice in Wonderland*; he has directed plays for the National, the Royal Shakespeare, and many other theatres; and he has directed opera in America, Australia, Britain, Germany and Italy. In addition to lecturing, he has written *The Body in Question* and *States of Mind*, both of which are based on BBC television series of the same name; *The Human Body* and *The Facts of Life*, both of which are popular books; and *Subsequent Performances*, published in 1986. He is currently Artistic Director of the Old Vic.

# List of contributors

**Hiram Brownell** is an Assistant Professor of Neuropsychology in the Department of Psychology, Boston College, Massachusetts, USA.

**Christie Davies** is a Professor in the Department of Sociology, University of Reading, UK.

**Nicholas Garland** is the political cartoonist for *The Independent*.

**Robert Goff** is a Professor in the Department of Philosophy and a Fellow of Cowell College in the University of California at Santa Cruz, USA.

**Alexander Kohn** is a Professor of Virology at the Tel-Aviv University Medical School, Israel.

**Michael Neve** is a Lecturer in the history of medicine in the Department of Anatomy and Embryology, University College London.

**Nicholas Tucker** is a Senior Lecturer in the Department of Psychology at the University of Sussex, UK.

**Richard Ward** is Director of Fool Time, The Centre for Circus Skills and Performing Arts, Bristol, UK.

# Introduction

## John Durant

Each summer, the British Association for the Advancement of Science convenes its Annual Meeting in a different university town or city. Typically, several thousand scientists, scholars, schoolchildren and interested members of the general public gather together for a week to attend a wide-ranging programme of lectures, seminars, visits and other activities relating to the worlds of science and technology. In the main, this programme is organized by a number of discrete sections, each of which is responsible for a particular scientific speciality – 'A' (Physics), 'B' (Chemistry), 'C' (Geology) and so on.

The one exception to this rule of subject specialization is named – significantly, according to Jonathan Miller in Chapter 1 of this volume – Section 'X', the 'General Section'. The task of Section X is to deal with things that are not subject-specific, either because they are intrinsically interdisciplinary, or because they have to do with the relationships between science and other aspects of our culture, such as the arts, or sport, or the military, or unemployment (all of which have been topics of Section X programmes during the past few years).

In 1987, the British Association travelled to Northern Ireland as guests of the Queen's University of Belfast. By common consent, the meeting as a whole was a great success; but those of us who work in Section X, in particular, were especially pleased with our programme, which dealt with the subject of humour. To be perfectly honest, we had not chosen this theme ourselves. Instead, and following a well-tried and proven formula, we had chosen a really excellent President for the year, and then left it to him to pick the theme.

When we invited Dr Jonathan Miller to be President of Section X, we had in mind the fact that he is one of the supreme generalists of the age. A trained scientist and physician, with special interests in psychology and neurology, he is also a successful popularizer of science, with a major BBC television series on human biology and many other programmes and books in this and related fields of science to his credit. As if all this were not enough, Jonathan Miller is also one of Britain's most respected theatre and opera directors, and he has recently been appointed Artistic Director of the Old Vic.

We had fondly imagined that Jonathan would choose as his theme for the Belfast meeting either a branch of medicine or something to do with the interface between science and the arts. What we had forgotten, however, was that his first really successful career had been as humorist in the early 1960s, when he played alongside Alan Bennett, Peter Cook and Dudley Moore in 'Beyond the Fringe'. This hugely successful review helped launch a new wave of satire; but it also aroused Jonathan's interest in the whole business of humour in general. What is a joke, and how does it work? What do people find funny, and why? Above all, why do people have a sense of humour at all?

This was the theme that Jonathan chose for Belfast. Over breakfast in London one Sunday morning, he told us that he wanted to take humour seriously. Instead of simply accepting as a mysterious gift one of the things that makes a human life worth living, he wanted, as it were, to put it under the microscope of scientific and scholarly scrutiny. Changing the metaphor, he wanted to see how the hand that works the puppet we laugh at actually works (see frontispiece illustration). Beforehand, we had, I confess, been a little nervous. Were there really important things to say about humour? And could they be said in a way that did not drain the subject of all interest, of all warmth, of all – well, humour?

Just listening to Jonathan outlining his plans, our fears rapidly melted away. One day would be spent looking at what jokes are, and at different theories of how they actually work. A second day would be spent looking at different social contexts of jokes and joking, including both the world of children's humour and the intriguing international phenomenon of the 'Irish joke' (we were, after all, going to be in Belfast). A third day would be devoted to 'non-verbal' humour – cartooning, clowning, mime and all the rest. And to cap it all, we would even find time to consider the role of humour in the generation of novel scientific theories. By the time breakfast was over, we knew we had a really marvellous programme in prospect.

This book is the outcome of a week in Belfast that more than lived up to our expectations. The chapters are based on the actual lectures themselves, as given to consistently large audiences in the Queen's University of Belfast. In addition to Jonathan Miller's opening presidential lecture (Chapter 1), there are contributions from academics (a historian, a philosopher, two psychologists and a sociologist), from a political cartoonist, from the director of a school for clowns, and from the editor of the *Journal of Irreproducible Results*. This mix of contributors gives some sense of the true interdisciplinarity of our subject-matter. Only by reading the book, however, is it possible to find out how much we learnt, and how much fun we had in Belfast.

# Chapter 1

# Jokes and joking: a serious laughing matter

Jonathan Miller     *Use in Ch.1 Humor.*

At the Manchester meeting of the British Association in 1842 a surgeon called James Bray tried to enter the topical but disreputable subjects of animal magnetism and mesmerism into one of the sections. He failed to gain admission and was forced to repair to the Free Trade Hall, where he was able to demonstrate the facts of mesmerism, which he then retitled hypnotism. (This was the occasion when the term 'hypnotism' was coined for the first time.) If a section labelled 'X' had existed in 1842, I have no doubt that the disreputable subject of animal magnetism would have succeeded in gaining admission. X is the lower end of the alphabet. X is a letter which is very rarely used, and then only for things that are out of the ordinary, out of the usual; for that which is in some way unclassifiable, or unmanageable. In his account of the concentration camps, Primo Levi recorded a hierarchy which existed among the inmates with regard to the numbers tattooed on their arms. Those with the lowest numbers, being the earliest arrivals, were the aristocrats; while those with the highest numbers, being the most recent arrivals, were the proletariat of the camp. In our case, X, General, represents the disreputable end of the British Association. It is the unclassifiable; that which is opposed to the pristine respectability of A, Physics, and B, Chemistry.

I think there is something quite significant about the fact that I am President of Section X, and that my subject is humour. For humour is an unclassifiable and an unmanageable subject, something which has consistently defeated the attempts of scientists to explain it. It also has other drawbacks as a subject for discussion. While it fails to gain admission for serious consideration by scientists, it is also regarded by those laymen who take great pleasure in the experience of laughter as being too frivolous and too enjoyable to be treated by science at all. In fact, the journalists who usually come to these meetings take great pleasure whenever someone does deal with humour in demonstrating how unfunny the treatment of the subject is; rather as if it should be a qualification of a surgeon dealing with cancer that he or she should have the disease before operating upon it.

Humour is an extremely difficult subject to talk about, and it is an even more difficult subject to be scientific about. We have to deal with the peculiar phenomenon of laughter, a respiratory convulsion which seems to be excited, whether we like it or not, by certain events which we experience. We normally regard laughter as an action, as something which we do; as a performance of some sort. But in fact it is hardly something in which we can be said to have competence. Laughter is not at all like a physical action: it is not like raising a hand, or making a fist; it is not like writing, or speaking. Laughter is not something which we can undertake voluntarily – we cannot laugh at will. Of course, we can put ourselves in situations where laughter is the result, but there is no way in which we can make ourselves laugh. Someone who does make him- or herself laugh – an actor or an actress, for example – is indulging in what we call mirthless laughter. True laughter is not something to which we have direct voluntary access.

In this sense, laughter seems to be a cognate concept with things like sneezing and coughing. We cannot sneeze at will; and once we have started to sneeze, we cannot always stop ourselves at will either. Similarly we cannot laugh at will; and once we have started laughing, we cannot always stop ourselves. In some ways, then, laughter has features in common with sneezing and coughing, in the sense that all of these things belong to the area of the involuntary. Yet in other ways they all belong to the province of the will. For example, we can voluntarily suppress sneezing, coughing and laughter. Thus, we may blame someone at a concert who sneezes or coughs, and we may blame someone at a funeral who giggles at the graveside. Thus, each of these phenomena is distinguished from other forms of involuntary action (such as peristalsis) that cannot be either started or stopped at will. Someone, for example, who at the graveside produces audible borborygmi may be laughable, but they are not blamable. We cannot be blamed for stopping peristalsis and we cannot be praised for starting it.

So we are dealing with actions that are involuntary, in the sense that they cannot be started at will; but that are voluntary, in the sense that they can be suppressed. Next, we must distinguish between involuntary actions like sneezing and coughing, on the one hand, and laughing and blushing on the other. We think of sneezing as being an involuntary action which can be induced by putting oneself in a situation which produces it. For example, we may take snuff in order to sneeze. Similarly with laughing and blushing. We have to put ourselves in situations where joking matter is around in order to make ourselves laugh, and we have to be in situations which are embarrassing in order to blush. However, there is a distinction between snuff and laughing matter, just as I believe there is a distinction between snuff and embarrassing matter. Snuff is a physical stimulus which attacks the nervous system from the 'bottom up', whereas laughing matter approaches the nervous system from the 'top down'. Snuff is purely physical; we do not have to understand anything in order to sneeze; but laughing matter is cognitive; we have to understand the situation before we can be tickled into laughter, or embarrassed into blushing.

It is interesting that we use the word 'tickling' because laughter does overlap into the sneezing area. We know that we can produce laughter by something as crude as a physical stimulus and this does not require cognitive appreciation in order to work.

So far, I have simply been exploring some concepts that are cognate with laughter. It may be worth recapitulating my main conclusions. Laughter is involuntary in the sense that we cannot start it, even though we can stop it. Laughter has to be started by putting oneself in a situation where the stimulus is provided. But the stimulus to laughter is not like the stimulus to sneeze. We do not have to be in a frame of mind in order to sneeze, we simply have to have our noses tickled. But a frame of mind is required for laughter. This is because laughter is a 'top-down' concept; in other words, it comes from higher, cognitive levels of the nervous system, as opposed to the other involuntary actions which attack the nervous sytem from the 'bottom up'.

The idea of laughter as a 'top-down' phenomenon can be demonstrated by an interesting clinical finding, which is taught to medical students when they go on the neurological wards and see patients with strokes. This finding is one of the ways in which we distinguish between an upper motor neurone and a lower motor neurone defect. The illness called Bell's Palsy attacks the seventh or facial nerve, and causes paralysis of one half of the face. In this palsy, half of the face becomes slack; patients may dribble from one side of their mouth, and often the lower eyelid is everted. Bell's palsy is an extremely painful and embarrassing affliction. However, it is what we call a lower motor neurone defect. It affects the lower part of the nervous system, the final common path through which motor impulses gain access to the muscles. In contrast, there are other, upper motor neurone defects which involve the same muscles. For example, a stroke which affects the motor neurones in the cerebral cortex may also cause paralysis on one side of the face. However, there are sharp distinctions in the repertoires of patients suffering from these two different sorts of defect.

We pick a patient with a stroke and ask them to show us their teeth. We say, 'Grin please', and they grin on just one side. We say for the second time, 'Grin, please, on both sides of your face.' Again, they respond by grinning on just one side. In other words, the patient does not have access to the other side of their face; not, that is, until we amuse them. Once amused, then there is bilateral symmetry in their performance. In other words, they do not have a total lack of access to their own face. They have access to their face with respect to a particular cognitive situation. If you amuse them, if they see a joke, they smile; but they cannot smile at will. In a patient with Bell's Palsy, a lower motor neurone defect, on the other hand, neither the order to grin nor amusement produces a symmetrical smile, because there is a block in the final path through which nerve impulses gain access to the relevant muscles.

The thing which is interesting here is the extraordinary situation of the stroke patient. He or she cannot grin to order, but they can smile when amused. This goes back to the question of how we gain access to involuntary performances like blushing and laughter, which seem to be things over which we have partial and incomplete control.

If a Martian visited the earth he, she or it would be extremely puzzled by the strange respiratory convulsion of laughter, which sometimes sweeps through assemblies, and which people pay large amounts of money in order to experience. This strange phenomenon, which has been called a sudden glory, cannot surely be a respiratory convulsion alone. After all, there are other ways of being convulsed respiratorily from which we actually flee. Indeed, we flee from the sort of laughter which we can be tickled into. This sort of thing can be torture, whereas no one ever flees from a cabaret or a performance of a great comedian. People flee from the laughter which is induced by physical stimulation, but no one flees from the laughter which is produced by a cognitive situation.

Now all of this leads us to ask an intriguing question: might there be some evolutionary significance in this curious performance of laughter; in this curious involuntary competence? Why is it that we pay so much money in order to put ourselves in situations where laughter results? Why is it that we pay so highly for people to do this to us, whereas we would not dream of paying someone to tickle our feet with a feather for three minutes? Could it be that there is an evolutionary pay-off in the pleasure which is associated with the cognitive situations which seem to induce this activity?

Presumably, there is a selective pay-off in the pleasure associated with sexual intercourse. If there were no pleasure to be associated with sexual intercourse we might forget to do it; in absent-mindedness, as it were, we might pass it up altogether. The same thing goes for eating; both sexual intercourse and eating involve the use of scarce resources, i.e. the resources of physical energy in the pursuit and the consummation of these activities. Both are selectively advantageous, and personally pleasurable. Without lapsing into the heresy of adaptationism — the assumption that every thing we do has some specific evolutionary pay-off – I would like to suggest that what is true of sexual intercourse and eating may also be true of laughter. In other words, I propose that there may be positive selective advantage associated with the cognitive rehearsals which we tend to go through in undergoing the experience of laughter.

To discover this evolutionary pay-off we must consider what laughter is for. There are many theories of the origins of laughter. In Chapter 3, Michael Neve deals with one of the most famous of these theories, which is Freud's idea that laughter is simply the release of repressed material which has been prevented from expressing itself. According to Freud, it is only through the medium of the joke, and suddenly, that repressed material is allowed us; and this provokes laughter. This is an idea which has gained wide acceptance in the psychoanalytic community, and I think there is something to be said for it; but I shall leave it to Michael Neve to explore this theory more fully.

Another, more biological, theory of laughter was proposed by the French philosopher Henri Bergson. Bergson claimed that we laugh at people in situations where they revert to a more automatic type of behaviour. When the herd observes a reduction in the versatility and flexibility of one of its members, it goes through loud respiratory convulsions which as it were ask the offending individual to 'pull its socks up'. A less flexible, less versatile individual endangers the biological integrity of the herd; and so the herd acts to protect itself. We laugh at the man who falls on the banana skin. (The man on the banana skin has become an emblematic figure in theories of humour, for reasons which have always escaped me.) Why? Because instead of retaining his versatility, his spontaneity and his flexibility, the man who tumbles is yielding to the force of gravity and is becoming something like a robot. He is becoming an inflexible object, and at that moment he is being reminded to pull himself together, to restore himself to a state of vigilant flexibility which will then make him into a valuable and productive member of the herd. Once again, it would be wrong to laugh this theory out of court; but as it stands, it deals with so little of the topic. This is a common feature of theories about humour: practically none of them cover the whole topic. There is almost always a series of exceptions which can be made to what purports to be a comprehensive theory of humour.

The last theory with which I shall deal very briefly is the idea that we laugh at situations where we see ourselves as superior to some victim. On this view, the victim of laughter is being reminded of his or her weakness by stronger members of the herd. In a performance that is an inheritance from our primate ancestors, dominant individuals put subordinates 'in their place'. This crude ethological view has been widely popularized; but I reject it out of hand because it overlooks complex cognitive and moral issues. This is why I prefer Erving Goffman to someone like Desmond Morris. Goffman perceived all of these things in their moral and social context, and not in terms of a crude inheritance from primate ancestors. Of course it may be possible to look at the motor performance of laughter and trace it back to certain primate roots; but at the cultural level I believe it has become latched on to something so elaborate, and so elaborately moral that it is no longer useful to consider it in crude ethological terms. This, I believe, is why Darwin's book on *The Expression of the Emotions* is such an intolerably tedious volume. It has encouraged even more tedious types of ethological thought in the last twenty-five years.

In contrast to all of these theories, I would like to raise what I believe to be a largely unconsidered theory of what humour is for, and what its biological value might be. In my view, the value of humour may lie in the fact that it involves the rehearsal of alternative categories and classifications of the world in which we find ourselves. Perhaps we should distinguish between serious discourse, on the one hand, and humorous discourse on the other (this is really a way to avoid using the word joke). When we are in the domain of humorous discourse – i.e. those cognitive situations which actually bring about laughter – we almost always encounter rehearsals, playings with and redesignings of the concepts by which we conduct ourselves during periods of seriousness. When we conduct our ordinary business in the world, our practical affairs, we deal with things for the most part by rule of thumb; we mediate our relationships with one another through a series of categories and concepts which are sufficiently stable to enable us to go about our business fairly successfully. But if we were rigidly locked on to these categories and concepts, if we were inflexibly attached to them, we would not continue to be a successful, productive and above all socially cooperative species. What we require, then, is some sort of sabbatical let-out in one part of the brain and one part of our competence to enable us to put things up for grabs; to reconsider categories and concepts so that we can redesign our relationships to the physical world, to one another, and even to our own notion of what it is to have relationships.

Perhaps I can illustrate this idea of what humour is for with a cartoon from the *New Yorker*. The cartoon portrays two African explorers in a swamp. They are wearing pith helmets, and are surrounded by lianas, creepers, serpents and so forth. They are obviously in trouble because they are up to their necks in the swamp as they proceed from left to right of the cartoon. The figure at the back is saying to the figure at the front: 'Quicksand or no, Carruthers, say what you like. I have half a mind to struggle.'

Simply describing the cartoon causes something strange to happen. Even without seeing the cartoon, we tend to laugh. Now, why is this? A crude, ethological view would be, 'Oh, we are taking pleasure by laughing at the fact that we are not in the swamp, and they are.' Or again, 'We are taking pleasure by laughing at what is clearly a ludicrous view of their true situation' I think, however, that if we parse the joke we can see that what is really going on is that certain categories with regard to the notion of volition are being played with. The cartoon actually throws up into the air the categories of will and action which we considered in relation to the notion of laughter as a voluntary or involuntary performance.

Consider the cartoon caption again: 'Say what you like, quicksand or no. I've half a mind to struggle.' Surely the core of this joke is not the situation of the swamp, nor the fact of our being outside the swamp and them being in it, but rather the fact that what we think of as struggling is not the sort of thing about which one could be in half a mind. We cannot as it were consider struggling as the next thing on the agenda. We cannot say: 'We've tried firing warning shots into the air; we've tried hanging on to the creepers; now let's have a spirited go at struggling'. Again, we laugh at the very thought of applying the notion of decision to something which is as it were a paradigm of those things to which we do not have voluntary access. Sneezing, laughter and struggling are not things which you can be in half a mind to do. Struggling is not even something which you can be in full mind to do. It is not something to which the notion of mind seems to be relevant at all. It is something which happens flat out, whether you like it or not. It is something about which, in retrospect (if the struggling worked), you might say, 'I'm afraid I found myself struggling, although I know I ought not to have done.' In exactly the same way, you might say at the graveside, 'I'm afraid I couldn't help myself laughing.' You cannot be in half a mind to laugh, but you can be in full mind to try and stop yourself laughing, and in much the same way you cannot be in half a mind to struggle but you can be in full mind to try and stop yourself struggling.

What I am suggesting is that this joke rehearses what we customarily think of as hard and fast divisions between the voluntary and the involuntary. In this way, it introduces us to a concept that is fundamental to our relationships with one another and to the organized structures of our society. One of the things which makes our society coherent is that we have notions of what it is meet to praise and what it is meet to blame; what we send people to prison for, and what we award them knighthoods for; what we hit them for, and what we kiss them for. In other words, we divide things into a series of praiseworthy areas and blameworthy areas. The *New Yorker* cartoon is one of a battery of jokes which plays with our notions of praise and blame. By applying these notions to something which is clearly in the area of the involuntary, this joke rubs our noses in some of the basic ideas by which we live. At the same time, it allows us to reconsider these notions, and (if appropriate) to revise them.

I would like to make use of another example before I close. Twenty-seven years ago, when I started out in the humour business, I performed for three years in 'Beyond the Fringe'. Each night, I used to stand open-mouthed with wonder at my colleagues performing on the stage and making other people laugh. I was always amazed at their talent, but also I was amazed at the relationship between their performance and the strange noise of laughter that came from the audience beyond the footlights. After three years, I was able to analyse the performance in some detail, and it was here that this notion of humour as a disorder of categories came home to me. I would like to give you one example from a sketch which we used to perform every night. It was a sketch about civil defence in which there were three of us behind a table, and Dudley Moore was planted in the audience to ask questions. The question of civil defence was raised and discussed, and half-way through we issued an invitation for questions from the audience, hoping, of course, that Dudley would get in first. Dudley would say, 'Yes, I have a question. Following the nuclear holocaust, how soon will normal public services be resumed?' The answer to that was: 'That's a very fair question. Following Armageddon, we do hope to have public services working fairly smoothly pretty soon after the event. In all fairness, though, I ought to point out that it must needs be something in the nature of a skeleton service.'

Now there are several pieces of 'joke-work', as Freud would put it, here. All of them involve opportunities for us to throw previously rigid categories into the air, and thus to reconsider the concepts by which we think and live. The traditional explanation of this joke is black humour. We laugh at something which is so intolerable, so horrible in our predicament that we simply have to laugh in order not to cry. This is one of the traditional sort of push-me-pull-you views of humour, which does not help at all. Much more plausible, I think, is the idea that the joke involves a subversion of our concept of Armageddon. Armageddon is not one of those things, like Christmas, or Thursday, which has events following it. It is not something which you might, as it were, put in your diary; so that in response to the question, 'What are you doing November 11th?', you could say, 'Well, I've got Armageddon coming up; but once that settles down ...'. Armageddon just is not something which settles down, or which has a sequel to it.

Just as struggling is not the next thing on the agenda, so Armageddon is not an event after which there can be other events, least of all, normal public services. Once again, I think, we are amused by a discrepancy; that is, the discrepancy between the magnitude of Armageddon in the form of a nuclear holocaust, and the extraordinary triviality of public services.

I would like to conclude with a well-known sequence in a Charlie Chaplin movie. All of us remember *The Gold Rush*. In that movie, there is a scene in which Charlie is starving in a hut and is forced to eat his boots. The audience becomes hysterical at certain points only, and these are points where the categories are in danger. The audience laughs at the moment when Charlie twists his bootlaces around his fork and treats them as spaghetti, and again at the point when he tentatively cuts the sole, tries a small piece of it, and savours it. Once again a discrepancy is the source of the joke. It is in the nature of boots that they are in the domain of the inedible. Here, however, someone is applying to the radically inedible the demeanour, the decorum and the finesse which normally apply to something that is the epitome of the edible; in this case, spaghetti and a very finely broiled steak. In this scene, we are being brought face to face with categories by which we live.

This example takes us back to the issues raised by Mary Douglas in her book *Purity and Danger*. There, Mary Douglas talks about the distinction between the dirty and the clean, the pure and the dangerous. Boots are things which belong on the floor, and they become dirty when they arrive on the table. In exactly the same way, what makes us laugh in the scene from *The Gold Rush* is the jarring discrepancy in which an object is suddenly and forcefully reclassified by being taken out of the category of the radically inedible and placed into the category of the finely, the wonderfully edible. Once again, this scene rejuvenates our sense of what these everyday categories are.

The rehearsal of categories in humour need not necessarily entail their revision. The point about such rehearsals is not that they have short-term consequences or benefits, but rather that they allow us to play with concepts and categories and thus to put joints into life. We may not be faced with the possibility of having to eat boots. Nevertheless, by having gone through the delightful experience of humour, we have prevented ourselves from becoming the slaves of the categories by which we live. This is why humour is so often regarded as a dangerous and even a subversive thing. The joker and the satirist are regarded as dangerous fellows; and the card in the pack which upsets the hand is called the wild card, or the joker. I think what we are seeing here is notion of the jocular as a kind of sabbatical section of the mind in which 'off duty' is celebrated. Being off duty is bound up with refreshment and recreation. I would remind you that recreation is in fact re–creation. It is the rehearsal, the re-establishment of concepts.

In all procedures of life there are rules of thumb which enable us to go on to 'automatic pilot'. I am not suggesting that these rules of thumb are bad. Far from it, they are necessary labour–saving devices which give our activities some sort of momentum. We depend on the existence of these categories in order to go about our everyday business. Jokes allow us to stand back from these rules and inspect them. Anthropologists make a distinction between serious and humorous discourse, and Edmund Leach distinguishes between sacred and profane time. There is a time in which we conduct our normal business, profane time. But there are always interludes in which the normal categories, social and otherwise, are suspended for the express purpose of undergoing sabbatical subversion. At Christmas time, for example, everything is up for grabs, and things are turned upside-down. (The historian Christopher Hill uses the phrase, 'a world turned upside-down', in connection with the English Revolution.) At Christmas time the pantomime dame is played by a man, the principal boy is played by a girl, masters serve and servants sit at table, a lord is crowned Lord of Misrule, a bishop is made of a boy, and so on and so forth. In short, the world is briefly and safely subverted in carnival time, in festival time, in order to allow us briefly to rehearse and revise the categories by which we live for the rest of the year. When the new year comes, and we undertake the incumbencies and offices of ordinary life, we do so hopefully, in the knowledge that the categories and concepts by which we have lived in the previous year have undergone some sort of revision. Through humour we are not so much the slaves of the rules of life as the voluntary survivors of them. So perhaps there is something in Bergson's idea that humour restores us to the more versatile versions of ourselves, so that in joking we may be undertaking the most serious thing we do in our lives!

# Chapter 2

# Neuropsychological insights into humour

## Hiram H. Brownell and Howard Gardner

Humour provides an effective means of communicating a range of ideas, feelings and opinions. Additionally, a sense of humour adds immeasurably to one's enjoyment of life and, especially, the company of others. These aspects of humour ensure that any disruption of a person's ability to understand or produce humour will have a marked effect on his or her quality of life. In this chapter, we shall discuss the ways in which a person's sense of humour can break down as a result of injury to the brain, and how these impairments can affect the ways in which such a person interacts with the world.

The work which we shall describe comes from the field of cognitive neuropsychology. Researchers in this field use the effects of brain damage as a means of investigating human understanding, or cognition. Typically, we test patients who have sustained damage to some specifiable portion of the cerebral cortex as a result of a stroke. Strokes occur when the blood supply to some part of the brain is cut off. This can happen if a blood vessel becomes occluded, thereby stopping the oxygen supply to a region of the brain. As a result of oxygen starvation, the tissue served by that blood vessel soon dies. Obviously, destruction of significant amounts of brain matter causes intel-

lectual decline. What is critical to cognitive neuropsychology is
that the effects of focal brain damage are often highly selective.
In other words, brain damage can leave a patient severely
impaired in one area of cognition, such as understanding jokes,
but leave the same individual normal or almost normal in other
areas, such as understanding the syntax of sentences or how
words refer to objects in the world.

The selectivity of the impairments resulting from focal brain
damage is important for several reasons. First, there is the
question of localization of function. If damage to one part of the
brain consistently yields a particular type of deficit, then one
can reasonably infer that the region is centrally involved in that
function. For example, if patients with damage to the right
cerebral hemisphere uniformly demonstrate a deficit in understanding jokes, then that region is probably required for processing relevant to humour comprehension.

Second, selective impairments provide a means of building
and testing theories about domains within cognition. For example, we might posit the existence of a basic humour centre in the
brain which, when injured, will limit a patient's ability to
understand any form of humour. A more likely possibility,
though, is that different forms or aspects of humour require
different skills. By studying selective impairments, we can
state a theory or model of humour that specifies relevant distinctions, and then test whether injury to specific portions of the
brain (such as the cortex in one or the other hemisphere) causes
disabilities that parallel the proposed distinctions. In other
words, the dissociations among abilities revealed by selective
impairments resulting from brain damage can both suggest and
confirm theoretical distinctions by showing that, in fact, the
brain honours just those distinctions. The approach has been
used extensively to investigate a variety of topics including
reading, memory, mental imagery, language processing and
even artistic ability (cf. Ellis 1982; Heilman and Valenstein
1985).

A third and last reason for studying the selective effects of
brain damage is clinical. Appropriate management of a patient
requires knowing which abilities are impaired by a given injury, and which are (largely) spared. This information provides
a basis for deciding, for example, which therapies are likely to

be of benefit in particular cases, as well as for resolving questions such as whether a patient can live at home or should be placed in an institution.

This brief introduction to the purposes of cognitive neuropsychology implies that this approach has a great deal to contribute to the study of humour. Understanding this contribution requires some familiarity with the clinical profile of patients with significant amounts of cortical damage in the right cerebral hemisphere. These patients present an unusual set of characteristics. Most often, their basic linguistic abilites are intact: they are not aphasic (i.e. lacking speech), and typically they have little trouble naming objects or understanding the syntax of sentences. However, they often (though not always) exhibit a range of other impairments. First, in terms of production, right hemisphere damaged (RHD) patients show poor judgement and insight into their problems; routinely, their discourse and actions are socially inappropriate. For example, one patient repeatedly referred to his wife – in her presence – as 'the old sow', and interrupted formal testing to ask the female examiner about her sexual activities the previous weekend. Frequently, patients are garrulous, and prone to making tangential comments (Gardner *et al.* 1983; Weylman, Brownell and Gardner, in press). When listening to some of these patients, one often wants to laugh because the comments are funny, though in a crude way. What is not clear is whether the patients are fully aware of either the humorous or the offensive potential of their comments.

Patients with right hemisphere disease are also impaired in understanding the discourse and actions of others. They have trouble understanding jokes told by other people, and also often miss the gist or main point of a conversation or story. It seems that RHD patients understand what is explicitly stated, but have trouble extracting appropriate inferences and nuances from communicative exchanges. They have been shown to misunderstand sarcasm and indirect requests (Foldi 1987; Hirst, LeDoux and Stein 1984; Jacobs, Brownell and Gardner 1985; Weylman *et al.*, submitted). For example, if a patient has the volume of the television turned up very loud, and someone says to him or her, 'I'm really glad you have the volume turned up so high', the patient might say 'Fine', never appreciating the sarcasm behind the other person's utterance or the indirect request to turn the volume down.

Depending on the location and extent of the lesion, RHD patients may also exhibit emotional or affective deficits (Tuckers 1981), as well as impairments in understanding or producing the accents and rhythms of speech (Heilman *et al.* 1984; Ross 1985). They may experience paralysis or weakness of the left side (arm, leg), and visual perceptual problems especially in the left visual field (Adams and Victor 1981). They may even show 'left neglect', i.e. a tendency to ignore objects in the left half of visual space. For example, a patient with profound left neglect may eat the food on the right side of a dinner tray, leave the food on the left side, and complain of still being hungry. At times, patients also exhibit denial of illness (anosognosia). For example, if a patient has a paralysed left arm as a result of a stroke he or she may deny it, saying that the arm is just tired. Sometimes a patient will even claim that a non-functioning left limb belongs to someone else. (Weinstein and Kahn 1955). In talking to an RHD patient, one often has the sense that the brain damage has altered in significant ways his or her personality.

Clinical observation strongly suggests that it is the right cerebral hemisphere which is especially relevant to humour competence, since one does not routinely see the same garrulous, socially inappropriate behaviours in patients with unilateral left hemisphere damage. Left hemisphere damaged (LHD) patients are typically aphasic; that is, they have marked disorders of language involving syntax, phonology or lexical semantics. There are considerable differences in linguistic abilities, depending on which portion of the left hemisphere is damaged (Hécaen 1979). What is notable is that LHD aphasic patients give the impression of being very aware of their social environment. Their discourse and actions are as appropriate as can be expected, given their language disturbances. They are sensitive to their deficits, and use a variety of compensatory strategies. When talking to an LHD patient, one typically has the sense that brain damage has seriously impaired the person's linguistic abilities, but has not drastically altered the underlying personality.

In comprehension, also, aphasic patients often show a level of understanding that is surprising in light of their basic linguistic deficits. They are often able to extract the gist or main point of a story or conversation, even when the syntactic structure of any single sentence might elude them. To support their language understanding, aphasic patients also tend to take advantage of whichever linguistic and paralinguistic cues are available. In general, the more context that is provided for an aphasic patient, the better he or she will understand (Gardner *et al.* 1983; Weylman, Brownell and Gardner, in press).

At this point, a couple of general points are in order. First, all of these clinical descriptions of patients are generalizations. Not all RHD patients exhibit all of the symptoms described, but many do have an aberrant sense of humour. These patients, therefore, provide an ideal population for investigating both the components of humour and the relationship between humour competence and performance in other domains, such as understanding non-humorous language. Second, we have not found evidence for a 'humour centre' in the brain. Rather, normal ability in the domain of humour requires component skills which are also important in other domains. Thus, the aberrant sense of humour in RHD patients is best explained as resulting from a variety of deficits. This conclusion fits well with the goal of cognitive neuropsychology: the identification of the component parts of complex, and often intriguing, human abilities.

In work conducted over several years, we and several colleagues (Amy Bihrle, Dee Michel, Heather Potter, John Powelson and Sally Weylman) have conducted experiments that go beyond the clinical descriptions offered above. Most of our work has involved the examination of deficits in humour comprehension, and specifically the comprehension of verbal short-story jokes. One goal of this work is to test whether RHD patients show selective deficits that can account for a portion of their troubles and that illuminate component processes we all use to appreciate jokes. In the final part of this chapter, we will discuss briefly the production of humour.

The following example taken from a recent study illustrates two components required for a successful short-story joke (Brownel *et al.* 1983).

> 'The neighbourhood borrower approached Mr Smith one
> Sunday afternoon and inquired, "Say, Smith, are you using
> your lawnmower this afternoon?"
> "Yes, I am," Smith replied warily.
> Then the neighbourhood borrower replied, "Fine, then you
> won't be wanting your golf clubs. I'll just borrow them."'

This and the other examples we have used are perhaps not exceptionally good jokes, but they are appropriate to the purposes at hand. They are readily identifiable by virtually any adult as examples of a common type of joke. Furthermore, they lend themselves to experimental manipulation, and thus can be used to reveal a great deal about humour.

Several scholars in different disciplines have identified two components of the joke as a unit of discourse, i.e. as a narrative form (e.g. Suls 1983). We have labelled these components 'surprise' and 'coherence'. A joke begins by establishing an expectancy in the opening lines. Listening to the beginning of a joke, a subject uses his or her knowledge of the world to predict what should happen next. The punch line, however, is surprising in that it violates the expectancy. Upon hearing the punch line, the subject realizes that his or her prediction has been disconfirmed and that the punch line is incongruous. After that realization, the subject must work to establish the coherence of the punch line with the beginning of the joke. The subject reinterprets the punch line by figuring out how it might fit with the beginning of the joke after all. Indeed, the success of a joke rests on the 'goodness of fit' between the punch line and what has come before, once the initial incongruity has been appreciated.

In the present example, the expectation is that the neighbourhood borrower wishes to borrow Mr Smith's lawnmower. However, the neighbourhood borrower disconfirms the expectation by asking to borrow a different item. Once the incongruity of the unanticipated request has been appreciated, the listener then figures out how the unexpected request fits in with what has come before. The borrower was aware of his reputation, and only focused on the lawnmower to start with in order to trick Mr Smith into having to loan the golf clubs.

By designing a 'joke completion task', we were able to test the ability to RHD patients to handle these two aspects of short-story jokes; the appreciation of surprise, and the ability to establish coherence by reinterpreting punch lines. In this experiment, subjects were presented with the beginning of a joke and then asked to select the correct ending from a set of alternatives. The alternatives were designed to test for a selective deficit relevant either to incongruity or to coherence.

The major types of alternative endings for the neighbourhood borrower joke are shown below.

Correct punch line:
*'Fine, then you won't be wanting your golfclubs. I'll just borrow them.'*

The correct punch line ending is surprising, but still makes sense when reinterpreted.

Straightforward ending:
*'Do you think I could use it [the lawnmower] when you're done?'*

The straightforward ending is the sort of matter-of-fact continuation one would expect on the basis of world knowledge. Accepting this alternative as providing an adequate completion to the joke suggests a failure to appreciate the role of surprise in short-story jokes.

Non sequitur:
*'You know, the grass is always greener on the other side.'*

The *non sequitur* ending is surprising and thus satisfies one requirement of the joke as a narrative form. However, it really does not make any sense in terms of what has come before in the joke. Accepting this alternative as an adequate completion suggests a failure to reinterpret the punch line to make it fit with the rest of the joke; in other words, it reflects a coherence deficit.

In this and subsequent studies, the performances of a small group of RHD patients (twelve in this case) were compared to those of a comparable group of non-brain-damaged control subjects. The RHD patients were all right-handed adult men less than seventy years of age who had suffered unilateral right hemisphere damage due to stroke. In general these patients had secondary (high school) educations.

The control subjects, drawn from the same general population as the stroke patients, were adult men less than seventy years of age without significant neurological histories. The reason for our using only male subjects is a practical one. This research was carried out largely in a Veterans Administration Medical Centre, which provided much easier access to male than to female subjects. We have no reason to think that qualitatively different results would obtain with female patients and control subjects.

The procedure a subject was asked to follow was intentionally kept simple. The subject was asked to pick the funny ending, i.e. the one that made the best joke. The examiner read the beginning of a joke (minus the punch line) to the subject. A card with the alternative endings was then given to the subject, and the examiner read each ending to the subject. After listening to all the alternatives, the subject indicated his choice.

The results supported the componential view of joke comprehension outlined above. Overall, the RHD patients scored worse than the control subjects. This, however, was to be expected; patients with significant amounts of brain damage should do worse than neurologically intact subjects. More relevant is that the RHD patients exhibited a selective deficit that compromised their understanding; that is, only one of the two components of this form of humour was affected by right hemisphere brain damage. This selective deficit was reflected in RHD patients' abnormal predilection for a certain type of error. Statistical analysis of subjects' errors revealed that the RHD patients were reliably more likely than the control subjects to choose the (incorrect) *non sequitur* endings. The patients were not noticeably different from the control subjects in terms of their attraction to the (incorrect) straightforward endings. Our interpretation of this finding is that the RHD patients were deficient in just the coherence requirement of jokes. Because they were impaired in their ability to reinterpret punch lines, the nonsensical *non sequitur* endings and the correct punch lines were more or less equivalent. Furthermore, the RHD patients had a preserved sense of what is required to make a joke. They retained the knowledge that jokes as a narrative form require a component of surprise. Accordingly, the RHD patients were not measurably confused by the straightforward endings, which lacked this component.

The first study left unresolved several issues that we shall now discuss in turn. First, is the deficit observed in RHD patients attributable to specifically right hemisphere damage, or, alternatively, would analogous deficits arise subsequent to brain damage irrespective of locus? To answer this question, we used a different kind of stimulus. Due to the considerable linguistic demands of the joke completion task, we were unable to test the best control group for general effects of brain damage: LHD aphasic patients. However a later study (Bihrle *et al.* 1986) investigated the same issues with both RHD and LHD patient groups. This follow-up study used verbal short-story jokes, as in the first study by Brownell *et al.* (1983); but in addition, the study included captionless, four-frame cartoons that were comparable to the short-story jokes in that they involved surprise and coherence. For both the verbal and the cartoon versions of the joke completion task, alternative endings were designed that selectively tapped appreciation of surprise and coherence. Because of the non-verbal nature of the cartoon task, it was possible to test LHD aphasic patients as well as (non-aphasic) RHD patients on this portion of the study. The LHD patients were not tested on the verbal task. (Non-brain-damaged control subjects were also tested, but these subjects found both tasks too easy and scored at near-perfect levels.)

The following is an example of a stimulus item from the verbal task along the most important ending types. It is important to note that there is a type of ending (the humorous *non sequitur*) that was not included in the first study.

'*A man went up to a lady in a crowded square. "Excuse me,"
he said, "Do you happen to have seen a policemen anywhere
around here?"
"I'm sorry," the woman answered, "but I haven't seen a sign
of one."
Then the man said, . . .*'

Correct punch line:
'*All right, hurry up and give me your watch and pocketbook
then.*'

The correct punch-line ending, of course, satisfies both the surprise and the coherence requirements.

Straightforward ending:
*'Damn, I've been looking for a half-hour and can't find one.'*

The straightforward ending is coherent but not at all surprising.

Neutral non sequitur:
*'Baseball is my favourite sport.'*

The neutral *non sequitur* ending is surprising but incoherent, since it could not be reinterpreted to make it mesh with the beginning of the joke.

Humorous non sequitur:
*'All of the wheels fell off my car.'*

The humorous *non sequitur* ending is surprising but incoherent. In addition, though, it is humorous in and of itself owing to its slapstick content. The humorous *non sequitur* endings were designed to convey humour that did not require the cognitive process of revising one's interpretation of a final sentence in order to integrate it with what had come before. Instead, appreciating the humour in these endings required only a superficial treatment of the stimulus, i.e. treating the ending (or, in the cartoon task, the final frame) as a single, unrelated entity.

The task was similar to that used in the first study: a subject had to pick the ending that would make the best (funniest) joke. Groups of RHD patients and LHD patients were tested in the cartoon task. The RHD patients were also tested in the verbal task.

The results were revealing in several respects. First, the major findings in both the verbal and cartoon tasks replicated the results of the earlier study (Brownell *et al.* 1983). The RHD patients showed a preserved sense of the role of surprise in this form of humour, but failed at the coherence requirement. That is, the RHD patients often confused *non sequitur* endings with

funny, correct endings, but they d
straightforward endings with funny

Of particular interest is the fact t
tients did not show the same types of e
The LHD patients more often confu
endings with the correct endings, and
*non sequitur* endings with the correc
different pattern of error tendencies su
deficit is specific to right hemisphere
appear to be a general result of brain d
age alone is not sufficient to produce a m…ᴋᴇᴅ attraction to *non sequitur* ending types.

The preliminary nature of this conclusion regarding localization of function warrants additional comment. In future work, it will be important to test whether these patterns of errors are primarily associated with damage to regions within the right (or left) hemisphere. One likely candidate is damage to the frontal lobes. To date, our studies have not provided any support for a special role for the frontal lobes (Bihrle *et al.* 1986), but this represents a null result that is difficult to interpret with confidence. These investigations have examined only one of the possible lesion sites within either hemisphere. For example, the effects of prefrontal damage – damage to the most anterior portions of the frontal lobes – have not yet been examined. There is a practical limitation in this work: the selection of specific lesion sites available for study is dictated by the distribution of the blood vessels (the middle cerebral arteries) that typically give rise to strokes.

A second unresolved issue concerns possible distinctions among types of humour distinguished in terms of their cognitive requirements and with respect to the regions of the brain needed to appreciate them. To support the importance of these distinctions, it would be important to assess what kinds of humour are still within RHD patients' grasp, in addition to showing what sorts of humour they fail to understand.

The results of our second study suggest one type of humour to which RHD patients are still sensitive: slapstick humour, such as that contained in the humorous *non sequitur* ending types. Of all the incorrect ending types, RHD patients were most attracted to the humorous *non sequiturs* when trying to con-

e. (The LHD patients were least attracted to humor-
*sequiturs*.) These endings did not require any integra-
of their content with the beginning frames of a cartoon
p, and were therefore funny in and of themselves. In this
respect, the humour was of a cognitively simpler sort than that
required for appreciation of the (correct) punch line. The RHD
patients' attraction to the humorous *non sequiturs* represents a
piecemeal approach to understanding humour and a consequent
failure to reinterpret a final frame or punch line. Thus, these
patients are not totally barred from appreciation of humour, but
rather appear limited in the types of humour they can readily
understand. In other words, there is neuropsychological support
for a distinction among genres of humour based on whether or
not a revision/reintegration process is needed.

A third issue arising from our first study is whether cognitive
deficit in reinterpretation is specific to humour, or instead represents a more general cognitive problem. The best answer at
present is that the same deficit that limits RHD patients' comprehension of punch lines also appears to affect their interpretation of other narrative units. In a more recent study (Brownell *et
al.*, 1986), we have demonstrated that the problem of reinterpreting a critical sentence also disrupts comprehension in a
non-affective, non-humorous context. In this study of inferenc-
ing capacity, subjects were asked to listen to pairs of sentences,
to treat them as single 'stories' or events, and to answer questions based on their understanding. Consider the following example:

Sally brought a pen and paper with her to meet the famous
movie star. The article would include comments on nuclear
power by well-known people.

After the first sentence, a normal listener makes the natural
inference that Sally is an autograph hound seeking a celebrity's
signature for her collection. However, after hearing the second
sentence in the same discourse, the listener must abandon this
initial interpretation, reinterpret his or her initial (incorrect)
inference, and construct a new understanding based on the two
sentences together, i.e. that Sally is a journalist writing an
article. The reinterpretation process is critical.

To assess subjects' abilities to perform this revision, vignettes such as the one shown above were presented along with a set of true–false questions designed to test subjects' understanding. The true–false questions for the sample vignette are provided as illustrations. One question always queried the 'incorrect inference' that one would make on the basis of the misleading information contained in the first sentence alone. Thus:

*Incorrect inference:*
Sally was going to ask the movie star for her autograph.

Another true–false question always queried the 'correct inference' that one would make on the basis of the two sentences together. Thus:

*Correct inference:*
Sally was going to interview the movie star for her article.

Two additional true–false questions for each vignette assessed subjects' comprehension and retention of the factual content of the vignettes. Performance on the fact questions was important since appropriate inferences would be possible only if the supporting information were available to subjects.

One other, critical aspect of the design of the study was that the misleading information was presented in the first sentence in half of the vignettes, and was presented in the second sentence in the remaining stimulus vignettes. Thus, the revision component was needed for only half of the items.

Subjects in this task were told to treat each pair of sentences as a single 'story' or event. The examiner read each vignette out loud as the subject read it to himself. The vignette was then removed from view, and the true–false questions presented one at a time. The subjects tested in this study consisted of a group of RHD patients and a group of non-brain-damaged control subjects drawn from the same general population.

The major results were that the RHD patients had considerable difficulty with the revision requirement. They were often stuck on the initial interpretation suggested by misleading information contained in the first sentence of a vignette. They fared much better when the misleading information appeared in the second sentence. Thus, the reinterpretation of an initial interpretation proved a significant obstacle to the RHD patients' comprehension. The control subjects did not show the same pattern. The implication of these results is that the humour deficit demonstrated in the verbal joke and cartoon tasks has been extended to another, less affective domain. Thus, the deficit does not seem to be specific to humour (i.e. there is no evidence from these studies for a 'humour centre' disrupted by unilateral right hemisphere damage). Similarly, the deficit does not stem from a pervasive affective disturbance.

Results from this set of three studies are consistent with the following account. Damage to the right hemisphere selectively affects patients' abilities to process one of two major components of humour: the ability to revise an initial interpretation in order to integrate a sentence (or final frame of a cartoon strip) back with what has come earlier in a discourse. This ability figures prominently in the comprehension of both humorous and non-humorous material. It seems to have some close connection to the right hemisphere, since we do not see the same deficits with damage to just any region of the brain. Finally, there is support for a separation among types of humour. The RHD patients seem to retain an appreciation of simpler, slapstick humour that does not require integration of content across sentences or across frames in a cartoon strip.

The final issue which we shall discuss concerns the production of humour. As we suggested at the beginning of this chapter, the production as well as the comprehension of humour is disrupted by damage to the right hemisphere. Although not nearly as much formal experimentation has been done to assess the productive capacities of patients, some promising leads are being developed. One broad topic concerns the narrative abilities needed to tell a successful joke. In our laboratory, we have begun to assess the production of jokes in a variety of ways. In a preliminary effort, RHD patients (and control subjects) were asked to tell one of their own favourite jokes and to retell jokes an examiner had just told them. In these tasks, the patients did fairly well, but they occasionally misordered or omitted key elements. Their difficulties in this highly constrained humour setting suggest a link between their humour production and deficits observed in the production of non-humorous narratives

(Delis *et al.* 1983; Gardner *et al.* 1983; Huber and Gleber 1982). Thus, narrative (or cognitive) problems of a general nature seem to affect humour output, which argues for viewing humour competence as a product of several component abilities that also figure in other, less affectively laden cognitive domains. Localization of these functions to the right hemisphere is difficult to assess because the linguistic demands of the tasks make testing LHD aphasic patients impractical.

Another component of successful humour production involves knowing when and where to tell a joke. What works in front of one audience, e.g. a group composed entirely of men, may not work at all in front of a mixed group of men and women. What might be safely and humorously said in private might produce awkward silence in a larger and more public setting. The sense of when it is permissible to say something involves judgement, the ability to inhibit oneself, and a degree of empathy. Even though preliminary, the scant empirical information available provides some insight into how these skills can be disrupted. The clinical profile presented at the outset suggests that right, but not left-sided pathology grossly alters a patient's sense of what is appropriate. The RHD patients are prone to making insensitive statements which can seem funny in some situations. In a comedy film, for example, a comment such as referring to one's wife as 'the old sow' might conceivably be thought funny; but in an actual situation in which someone's feelings are likely to be hurt, it is deadly serious.

In a study currently in progress in our laboratory, RHD patients are being asked what a person is likely to feel in certain situations, such as eating in a restaurant and having hot coffee spilled in one's lap by a waiter. Faced with this particular situation, some of the RHD patients tested to date have shown a tendency to answer 'hot and wet' rather than 'angry'. That is, they appear to focus on the physical events rather than the emotional sequelae of those events. This overly literal analysis of the environment is not likely to provide patients with an accurate sense of other people's emotional states. This test has not been administered to patients with left-sided brain damage, but clinically one would expect more sophisticated responses from LHD than from RHD patients. These deficits, though as yet poorly defined, suggest that a sense of social perspective and empathy is missing in RHD patients. The RHD patients may therefore have trouble judging when it is acceptable to tell a joke. These speculations, as well as related work by other researchers, suggest that this impairment in social perspective and empathy extends well beyond humour, limiting RHD patients' performance in other social and cognitive domains (Coslett, Bowers and Heilman 1987; Duncan 1986).

In conclusion, we have summarized some cognitive deficits that are associated with unilateral right hemisphere brain disease and that limit patients' humour competence in specific ways. Patients' ability to understand jokes is hurt by the difficulty they have in revising an interpretation of a punch line to achieve a coherent understanding of the whole joke. There is some evidence that comprehension of other, simpler forms of humour such as slapstick are less disrupted. The RHD patients' efforts at producing humour at appropriate times appear to be hampered by a deficit in social judgement. Taken together, these observations illustrate how the study of pathological populations may shed new light on important but still poorly understood aspects of the human experience.

## References

Adams, R. D. & Victor, M. (1981) *Principles of Neurology*, 2nd ed. New York: McGraw-Hill.

Bihrle, A. M., Brownell, H. H., Powelson, J. A. and Gardner, H. (1986) Comprehension of humorous and non-humorous materials by left and right brain damaged patients. *Brain and Cognition*, 5, 399–411.

Brownell, H. H., Michel, D., Powelson, J. A. and Gardner, H. (1983) Surprise but not coherence: sensitivity to verbal humor in right hemisphere patients. *Brain and Language*, 18, 20–7.

Brownell, H. H., Potter, H. H., Bihrle, A. M. and Gardner, H. (1986) Inference deficits in right brain-damaged patients. *Brain and Language*, 27, 310–21.

Coslett, H. B., Bowers, D and Heilman, K. M. (1987) Reduction in cerebral activation after right hemisphere stroke. *Neurology*, 37, 957–62.

Delis, D. C., Wapner, W., Moses, J. A. and Gardner, H. (1983)

The contribution of the right hemisphere to the organization of paragraphs. *Cortex*, **19**, 43–50.

Duncan, J. (1986) Disorganization of behaviour after frontal lobe damage. *Cognitive Neuropsychology*, **3**, 271–90.

Ellis, A. (ed.) (1982) *Normality and Pathology in Cognitive Functions*. London: Academic Press.

Foldi, N. S. (1987) Appreciation of pragmatic interpretations of indirect commands: comparison of right and left hemisphere brain-damaged patients. *Brain and Language*, **31**, 88–108.

Gardner, H., Brownell, H. H., Wapner, W. and Michelow, D. (1983) Missing the point: the role of the right hemisphere in the processing of complex linguistic materials. In E. Perecman (ed.), *Cognitive Processing in the Right Hemisphere*, pp. 169–91. New York: Academic Press.

Hécaen, H. (1979) Aphasias. In M. S. Gazzaniga (ed.), *Handbook of Behavioral Neuroscience*, vol. 2 *Neuropsychology*, pp. 239–92. New York: Plenum Press.

Heilman, K. M., Bowers, D., Speedie, L. and Coslett, H. B. (1984) Comprehension of affective and nonaffective prosody. *Neurology*, **34**, 917–21.

Heilman, K. M. and Valenstein, E. (eds) (1985) *Clinical Neuropsychology*. New York: Oxford University Press.

Hirst, W., LeDoux, J. and Stein, S. (1984) Constraints on the processing of indirect speech acts: evidence from aphasiology. *Brain and Language*, **23**, 26–33.

Huber, W. and Gleber, J. (1982) Linguistic and nonlinguistic processing of narratives in aphasia. *Brain and Language*, **16**, 1–18.

Jacobs, J. R., Brownell, H. H. and Gardner, H. (October 1985) Appreciation of sarcasm by right brain-damaged patients. Academy of Aphasia, Pittsburgh, Pennsylvania.

Ross, E. D. (1985) Modulation of affect and nonverbal communication by the right hemisphere. In M-M. Mesulam (ed.), *Principles of Behavioral Neurology*, pp. 239–57. Philadelphia: F. A. Davis.

Suls, J. M. (1983) Cognitive processes in humor appreciation. In P. E. McGhee and J. H. Goldstein (eds), *Handbook of Humor Research*, pp. 39–57. New York: Springer-Verlag.

Tucker, D. M. (1981) Lateral brain function, emotion, and conceptualization. *Psychological Bulletin*, **89**, 19–96.

Weinstein, E. A. and Kahn, R. C. (1955) *Denial of Illness, Symbolic and Physiological Aspects*: Springfield, Illinois: Charles C. Thomas.

Weylman, S. T., Brownell, H. H. and Gardner, H. (in press) 'It's what you mean, not what you say': pragmatic language use in brain-damaged patients. In F. Plum (ed.), *Language, Communication, and the Brain*. New York: Raven Press.

Weylman, S. T., Brownell, H. H., Roman, M. and Gardner, H. (submitted for publication) Appreciation of indirect requests by left and right brain-damaged patients: the effects of verbal context and conventionality of wording.

# Chapter 3

# Freud's theory of humour, wit and jokes

## Michael Neve

*Jokes and their Relations to the Unconscious* (and part of the interest in this text of Freud's is the difficulty of translating the title into English) appeared in 1905 as *Der Witz und seine Beziehung zum Unbewussten*. James Strachey's Englished attempt was published in 1916. The years preceding 1905 were vital to the development of Freud's views, after *The Interpretation of Dreams* (1900) and *The Psychopathology of Everyday Life* (1901). The book on jokes is easily overlooked, but fits with other Freudian preoccupations – dreams, for example, and the oddness of the everyday. The book raises quite important issues about the psychoanalytic project, and the idea that there might be something as sombre as a science of jokes, or of humour.

To put it harshly, or at its least dream-like, it may be that the science of jokes drives out the capacity to laugh. Freud's book, most readers (and there seem to be very few) agree, is not game for a laugh. Freud had a theory of jokes, but where, as it were, are the jokes? Of all the works of Freud's maturity, his book on jokes can lead one to fear that the psychoanalytic model slowly comes to replace the objects of its apparent concern: that the *real* joke is that objects of affection, objects of attention, objects of dreams or desire, objects of mirth; all of these start to be replaced by the theory (Freud's theory) of what, or who, they might be. Haunted, or troubled, somewhere in our ego or super-ego as to why we find jokes funny, or a particular person's jokes funny, we may end up being unable to laugh. We may end up, in the worst sense, taking ourselves seriously.

Now, as Jonathan Miller's contribution to this volume suggests, there may be aspects of jokes, of laughter, that could do with a bit of super-ego close down, since large parts of the public business of laughter are simply forms of garish stereotyping. Learning that what we are really doing in laughter is laughing *at*, in order to make the object of our laughter unhappy and reduced, is a real lesson. Laughing is the opposite of itself, or can be. Behind the cackle lurks the desire, lurks the intention, to hurt. This is a real possibility, and one authority for it is Darwin. In his book of 1872, *On the Expression of Emotion in Men and Animals*, Darwin sees many civilized expressions as a kind of darkness visible, as thin façades for more ancient, more bellicose feelings. Laughter may well be a civilized version of lethal instinct.

Freud's book raises issues like this, and, not least in the sorts of jokes that it uses as examples, leaves many readers cold. The joke that Freud may be playing on himself – that he is really mapping the collapse of his own sense of humour – can seem like a real one. And he has some striking things to say about the differences between types of joking (between 'the comic', for example, and 'humour') that illuminate the model of latent aggression. Along with other insights, these remarks of Freud have not been widely noticed, and this short essay will attempt to bring a couple of these hidden insights to light. But the first, and the important, impression of the book of 1905, and then 1916, is its dullness; its laboured, scientistic, ponderous examination of one of the most vivacious forms of libidinal release that, in the way endorsed by Michel Foucault, could most do with being left alone, happy to flourish outside the dead space of human scientific dissection, where the drive towards power and knowledge kills the thing it loves. But on rereading, indeed several rereadings, Freud's text also discovers other things, or so it seems to me, things that may rescue it from itself, so to speak, and which allow the reader to advance, rather than retard, the life of enjoyment without the knowledge of death.

It seems pretty clear, in terms of pure chronology, that Freud took up the question of jokes out of his previous studies on dreams, slips of the tongue, and the general question of the unruly relationship between dreaming, sleeping, repressing and forgetting that makes up what might be called everyday life.[1] Indeed, James Strachey tells us that while reading the proofs of *The Interpretation of Dreams*, Freud's (then) friend Wilhelm Fliess had complained that some of the dreams in that work were too full of jokes. No doubt, the nature and purpose of jokes had been on Freud's mind for some time.

Jokes, like dreams, and like parataxis or slips of the tongue, express repressed or unconscious wishes. And, as Freud rightly observes, the boundary of the joke, like the unconscious, is that it does not have one. Jokes contain brief, and sometimes abstract, chronicles of the time, and they also travel at a speed worthy of unconscious processes. Indeed, jokes universalize while at the same time allowing the individual a boastful relationship to having heard them since, in passing the joke *on*, the speaker gains certain satisfactions that are pleasing. Part of Freud's purpose is to ask what these satisfactions might be.

First, however, Freud examines 'the technique of jokes', breaking this down into condensation, multiple use of the same material, and double meaning (often with a play on words, or an allusion inside the double meaning). For condensation, Freud asks us to think of the remark of Thomas de Quincey, the English essayist, that old people are inclined to fall into their 'anecdotage'; or else the remark that, for many of us, our summer breaks are really 'alcoholidays'. The extension of this idea into the interest Freud shows in the sounds of words, which then leave meanings gliding into each other in funny, perhaps sinister ways, focuses on a quip on the treachery of translation: *traduttore–traditore*. These become, as it were, the same word, something that Strachey must have felt in attempting to translate Freud himself.[2] And then, certain jokes go on to make use of the same words that, by contrast, make (somewhat feeble) jokes: thus, Oliver Wendell Holmes: 'Put not your trust in money, but put your money in trust.'

Freud's interest in this 'use of the same material', by way of contradiction, is that it allows him to introduce his first great theme, of latent aggression. The contradiction within a sent-

ence can become a *tu quoque* between persons, a form of *repartee*.
Freud sees repartee as the place where the verbalization of
contradiction can begin, and the joke becomes a way of answer-
ing back. Thus, an innkeeper and a baker attack and counter-
attack. The innkeeper has a sore on his finger, and the baker
says, 'You must have got that by putting your finger in your
beer.' 'It wasn't that,' replied the innkeeper, 'I got a piece of your
bread under my nail.'[3] This unfunny exchange is a premonition
of the division into the purposes of some jokes as against others,
that is that some are 'abstract', they float, and some (which
Freud calls 'tendentious') contain purpose and point and are
likely to be either obscene or hostile. The place of hostility, in
the joke that is tendentious or more mildly, has allusion, pun or
double meaning in it, raises an issue that needs pondering.
Freud often tells Jewish jokes when looking at the place of
hostility in the joke world (as in two Jews outside the bathhouse:
'Another year gone by', one of them sighs), and many of Freud's
tendentious jokes, at least with regard to aggression, are Jewish. Why?

The historian of psychiatry, Sander Gilman, has attempted
an answer.[4] According to Gilman, Freud is pointing up, in the
Jewish jokes that he cites, the quality in them of *mauscheln*, or
the presence of Yiddish intonation in the German speech of
German-speaking Jews. The Yiddish accent makes the German
speech a less than pure sound, and thereby gives away the
speaker as being, by the presence of *mauscheln*, an outsider. As
Gilman puts it, in looking at Freud laughing *at* these jokes, 'The
object is the Eastern Jews who are trying to achieve status by
speaking German but who reveal themselves through the nature of their language.'[5] He goes on to suggest that the reason
both for this embarrassment and this interest, this concern to
identify with the joke in *mauscheln* and yet to keep separate
from it, is that all such jokes reminded Freud of his vulgar, but
comic, father, Kallamon Jakob Freud, whose jokes may have
been both provincial and, probably, sexual.

In terms of his division into the tendentious and the abstract,
Gilman is suggesting that in varying degrees hostility and
obscenity linger in the Jewish jokes that both appeal and interest Freud, and that they come to provide exemplary material
so that, in raising a laugh, they can be laughed at, as a form of

distance and distancing. Freud himself does not *tell* these jokes, because that would, according to Gilman, give him away as a provincial. Instead, he looks at Jewish jokes (and then jokes in general) through the gaze of psychoanalysis (i.e. 'science') and through the medium of his *mauscheln*-free German. Freud, according to Gilman, replaces the insecurities of the vulgar, *mauscheln* Jewish joke with the new language, and the new, non-provincial security and authority of psychoanalysis. In explaining the Jewish joke, Freud escapes its grasp, the grasp of his father and of low social status.

This is a bold claim. It helps the reader through the business of sorting out some of Freud's distinctions in the forms of jokes and joking, and especially the interest in the distinction between the abstract (or innocent), and the tendentious (or hostile/obscene) joke. Part of what I want to say here is that, as an argument, Gilman's conceals from the reader a further contribution that Freud wishes to make. An important analytical point here is that tendentious jokes do not, in Freud's account, merely give vent to hostility. They also give pleasure; indeed, they give pleasure in ways that abstract jokes cannot. Jokes with a point give most of themselves; their aim can be either aggressive, or more benign. But to portray the place of Freud's use of the Jewish joke as the site of a cultural distancing that psychoanalysis will provide is literally to disfigure the argument of *Jokes and their Relation to the Unconscious*. Without perhaps being able to complete the proposal, Freud has provided the attentive reader with a way out of the theoretical double bind (that is, the theorization of natural powers such that they disappear) which a case like that put forward by Gilman entirely misses. This is true even if, as Gilman sees it, Freud shares with other writers the view that women (and Jews) do not laugh, but rather mock.[6] Hence, in understanding 'jokes', Freud may be asking to be seen as superior to both. This still leaves Freud's deeper thoughts – his deeper gift – intact.

How does the argument proceed, allowing a reading of Freud's view of jokes less self-hating than that proposed by Gilman? Essentially, Freud proposes a kind of *scala naturae* for the joke, a series of kinds of purpose for jokes that goes from innocence (play, jesting) to tendentious jokes that have a true purpose, to amuse, or arouse, or versions of these. In the lowliest forms of joke (jest, the innocent joke) the source of pleasure is close to the abstract pleasure of nonsense. Innocence borders on nonsense; indeed, nonsense inhabits the land of innocence, and asks to be left unexamined. A certain silliness – a certain double-sided silliness of sound, for example – is the form of these jokes, remote from the aims of the tendentious joke, but no less confusingly pleasurable.

As Freud ascends his *scala naturae* of jokes, the reader begins to understand the structure of his argument. The more purposive the joke, the more pointed the joke, the more remote the joke is from the child's world of innocent play that lowlier forms resemble. Tendentious jokes have aspects that punning and word-play do not have: they can, for example, be cynical: they can attack actual forms of social institution. Thus: 'A wife is like an umbrella – sooner or later one takes a cab.'[7] Freud says of this example (from a Viennese carnival jest book) that the joke has, as it were, gone too far, to be replaced by mere cynicism.

This kind of joking has two aspects that make the *scala naturae* also a social scale. The jokes of innocence are aimless, based on sound difference, or word-play. The jokes of experience penetrate the social order, indeed they derive their particular force from opening up the social world by freeing repressed material and then making their comment (with purpose) on the world.

This group of distinctions allows Freud to make an important further point, which is the difference between the comical and the humorous. Humour, unlike the comic, is a kind of private satisfaction in Freud's terms; it involves a certain amount of social understanding, but can be shared by someone with themselves. The humorist chuckles to himself. The comic, on the other hand, is a broader category. In this (and here Freud takes up some ideas from Henri Bergson) someone else becomes laughable because they often seem to be overdoing something and then forgetting themselves, or running out of steam. Seeing someone trip over in the middle of a pretentious lecture; or hearing someone farting during prayers: this is the world of the comic, where the over-expenditure of effort, by someone else, is sabotaged by some mishap, leaving the object of comedy exposed to view with, as it were, all their apparatus on show.

Once again, the thing Freud is sorting out here is the relative publicity required for different effects, and for different kinds of

pleasure to occur: alone, or ̶ ̶ ̶ ̶ ̶ ̶ ̶ ̶ ̶ ̶ ̶ ̶ ̶ ̶ ̶ ̶
ting this, which we shall retur̶ ̶ ̶ ̶ ̶ ̶ ̶ ̶ ̶ ̶ ̶ ̶ ̶ ̶
their own jokes, either alone or ̶ ̶ ̶ ̶ ̶ ̶ ̶ ̶ ̶ ̶ ̶
are not actually funny; or at leas̶ ̶ ̶ ̶ ̶ ̶ ̶ ̶ ̶
course, at the top end of his scale ̶ ̶ ̶ ̶ ̶ ̶ ̶
interested in the varieties of aggressi̶ ̶ ̶ ̶ ̶
Here, cynicism may shade into degradati̶ ̶ ̶
degrade another. Indeed, certain jokes atte̶ ̶ ̶
persons, in public, in ways not unlike scenes ̶ ̶ ̶
of Ingmar Bergman. Here, the tendentious ̶ ̶ ̶ ̶
what might, ironically, be called its fully adult ̶ ̶ ̶ ̶ ̶ ̶ ger
private and humorous, no longer comic but u̶ ̶ ̶ ̶ ̶ ̶ed, but
rather fully armed, openly social, and with certain ɪatal long-
ings that do not even operate in the child's world at the other end
of Freud's scale of innocence.

This leads on to perhaps the nub of the argument in *Jokes and
their Relation to the Unconscious*. This is, not so much, 'what are
jokes', as '*who* are jokes for?' Anyone who has stayed loyal to
Freud's exposition up to this point is rewarded with a pleasurable insight that has too often gone unnoticed in studies of
Freud and jokes. For Freud, no true joke is alive, or even extant,
without someone (else) hearing it. Making fairly obvious analogies with the need for dream-work, and general symptoms of
psychological kinds to be seen (and heard), Freud takes proper
joking to be, not even a two-way, but a three-way, process. There
is the person who *has* the joke; there is the person who *hears* the
joke; and there is the person who can enjoy the joke *once* he has
told it. But none of this can happen unless the joke is heard,
because only then can the carrier of the joke, who gives pleasure
in telling the joke, experience the joke itself. The best joke-
tellers, and possibly the funniest people, avoid narcissism (and
laughing at their own jokes) but wait to give pleasure; pleasure
that is then returned as the joke takes its effect. The ego is at
work but on behalf, first of others and only then of itself. This is
a deeply pleasurable event, and distinguishes true wit from
something more introverted and possibly (as Hobbes suggests in
*Leviathan* about people laughing at their own jokes) totalita-
rian. As Richard Wollheim elegantly says of the joke that
works: 'A moment's mobility is granted to the mind.'[8] The comic,
and the humorous, can be private events; the good joke cannot.

that humour, the comic and the joke share
grees of privacy, varying degrees of innocence, and
ng degrees of purpose, either hurtful or restorative. But
he pleasure we may derive from his ideas on jokes comes from
other sources. For Freud, the person with a joke, and especially
the person (that rare creature) who has made up a joke, has
made this *for* someone. Someone, in the world, will bring this
joke to life (and thus bring to life the joke-bearer) by getting the
joke. It is a secretive, erotic bond that avoids the darker energies
of sexual action by (perhaps) being longer lasting and just as
important. Freud does not see his argument through, and his
book is dull; but he points the way. Jokes are forms of contact,
forms of knowledge. They are unlikely to be heard by people who
do not in some sense love us, just as it is unlikely that we really
love people who fail to make us laugh. Jokes, and the process of
joking, redeem sexuality by making light of it, while being
entirely dependent on an erotic bond to make them audible.

The lacunea in Freud's book are obvious. It is certainly surprising how little he says about people who say they can never
remember a single joke, itself a fascinating question, since it
suggests that they have never been encouraged to trust their
love, and hence their capacity to make the joke. And of course
there are people who do nothing but joke, and who may thereby
have lost their listeners, or listener, since the joke has to be
placed, has to be focused, in order to be heard. Nevertheless, by
making the social process the crucial question in the life of a
joke, Freud rescues his theory from determinism and scientific
annihilation, and keeps alive the idea that joking is a benign
form of love-making, to be protected against stereotyping and
degradation by the inventiveness of long acquaintance between
people no longer sexually enthralled. The jokes discussed elsewhere in this book – jokes of racist and sexist kinds – cannot, on
Freud's reading, be truly funny, since they have not made the
journey from childhood to shared pleasure that real jokes embody. Good joking, joking that does not wish death on others,
takes us back to what Freud calls 'the mood of our childhood'
when, with a minimum of effort, the unselfconscious pleasures
of noise and sound were experienced without too much fear.
Burdened by knowledge, adults – real adults – recover this
moment by trusting others to realize that they have become

funny, and going on to share that joke and its permanent, mild eroticism.

## Notes

1. The best account of this remains Richard Wollheim's, in his *Freud* (London: Fontana/Collins, 1971), pp. 65–106. There are a number of other specialized studies of Freud; some of Freud and jokes, but for brevity's sake I shall take my cue from Wollheim, whose short book remains an astonishing source of insight, albeit devoid of biographical or social-historical dimensions.
2. Freud, *Jokes and their Relation to the Unconscious*. London: Penguin Books, 1986, pp. 53 and 67.
3. Ibid., p. 107.
4. Sander Gilman, Sigmund Freud and the Jewish joke. In *Difference and Pathology*, pp. 175–90. Cornell, 1985.
5. Ibid., p. 185.
6. Ibid., p. 188. Gilman makes use here of the influential argument of Otto Weininger in his book *Sex and Character* of 1903, where women and Jews, as 'forms of nothing', cannot manage the disciplined civilities of joke-making and joke-telling.
7. Freud, op. cit., pp. 119 and 156.
8. Wollheim, op. cit., p. 105.

# Chapter 4
# The Irish joke as a social phenomenon

## Christie Davies

The first and most essential point to grasp in analysing the social significance of the Irish joke is that it is an international phenomenon. In a very large number of countries, essentially similar jokes are told about the alleged stupidity of a local ethnic or regional minority or neighbour.[1] Table 1 gives a partial list of such countries.

Table 1

| Country where jokes about stupidity are told | People *about whom* the jokes are told |
| --- | --- |
| Britain | Irish |
| United States | Poles (and locally other groups) |
| Canada (Ontario) | Newfoundlanders (Newfies) |
| Canada (West) | Ukrainians |
| Australia | Irish, Tasmanians |
| New Zealand (North Island) | Irish, Maoris |
| New Zealand (South Island) | Irish West Coasters |
| Ireland | Kerrymen |
| South Africa | Afrikaners (Van der Merwe) |
| France | Belgians, Swiss (Ouin-Ouin) |
| Netherlands | Belgians, Limburghers |
| Germany | Ostfrieslanders |

| Country where jokes about stupidity are told | People *about whom* the jokes are told |
| --- | --- |
| Sweden | Finns, Norwegians |
| Denmark | Jutes (from Aarhus) |
| Finland | Karelians |
| Italy | Southerners |
| Switzerland | Fribourgers |
| Greece | Pontians (Black Sea Greeks) |
| Austria | Carinthians, Burgenlanders |
| Yugoslavia | Bosnians, Albanians |
| Bulgaria | Sopi |
| Czech lands | Slovaks |
| Russia | Slovaks |
| Tadjikistan | Uzbeks |
| Turkey | Laz (from the region of Trebizond) |
| Iran | Rashtis (Azerbaigianis from Rasht) |
| Iraq | Kurds |
| Israel | Kurdish Jews |
| Egypt | Nubians |
| India | Sikhs (Sardarji jokes) |
| Mexico | Yucatecos (from Yucatan) |
| Brazil | Portuguese |
| Colombia | Pastusos (people of Pasto in Narino) |
| Nigeria | Hausas |

Clearly, jokes told about the stupidity of some other group have a near-universal popularity. Such jokes provide the tellers with a sense of sudden playful superiority which seems to be the essence of much humour generally.[2] In the days when people had a *local* rather than an ethnic identity, such jokes about stupidity were told about the inhabitants of particular 'fool towns' or villages, of which there were many – Abdera in ancient Greece, Cumae in southern Italy, Cuneo in northern Italy, Schilde (Laleburg) and Teterow in Germany, Ratot in Hungary, Pitsilia in Cyprus, Gotham in England, the imaginary Jewish Chelm, etc.[3] Some of these jokes about towns and villages survive today in countries where local identities are still important (for instance, they are still told about Homs and Hama in Syria), or where a town (such as Rasht or Aarhus) can be made to stand for the larger group.

Irish jokes have a very good comic structure, for they are based on a well-known standard script capable of infinite subtle varieties – the script of stupidity.[4] The use of an *ethnic* group to introduce the stupidity script is ideal from the point of view of comic structure, for it conveys just the right amount of information to enable the audience to understand that a particular kind of joke may be in the offing, but not so much information as to destroy the ambiguity and suspense necessary for all jokes. A French joke that begins: 'Two Belgians were travelling from Brussels to Paris ...', presents a French audience with a statement which has two well-recognized meanings; it *could* be the beginning of a true story about real people from Belgium *or* it could be the start of an ethnic joke about stupidity. The audience is thus alerted that a joke about stupidity may be told, but (especially if the raconteur tells it with a straight face) they are not certain of this until the arrival of the punch line. Only then is the ambiguity resolved and the suspense relieved in laughter.

The full force of this point can be seen if we try to rewrite such a joke to make it either more explicit or more disguised. If the joke were to begin: 'Two *morons* were travelling on a train to Paris ...', then the idea of stupidity would be introduced far too directly and obviously at the very beginning of the joke. Perhaps this is why jokes formulated in this way have never had a lasting popularity.[5] A different kind of problem would arise if the joke began: 'Two men were travelling on a train to Paris ...', or even: 'Two Scotsmen/Swedes/Japanese/Canadians were travelling on a train to Paris ...', because for a French audience these introductions do not evoke a possible stupidity script. In consequence the listeners may fail to see that a joke has been told at all, and simply see it as a pointless anecdote full of sound, if not fury, and signifying nothing. The phrase 'Two Belgians' is ideal because it is compatible with two opposed scripts, a real script about real Belgians and a conventional script about comic stupidity. The balance between the two is maintained until the punch line, when a rapid switch to the latter interpretation is unleashed. The mask of Janus is suddenly removed to reveal the mask of comedy beneath.

I have outlined how a joke based on a conventional ethnic script about stupidity works, but by tacit agreement a French joke-teller and his or her audience have many other ethnic scripts they can use about boastful Americans, canny Scotsmen or Auvergnats, stand-offish Englishmen, cunning Jews, cowardly Italians, militaristic Germans, and many others. In each case there is a cultural convention, a comic *blason popu-laire*, a simple formula that enables the jokes to work. In princi-ple, it is no different from the comic conventions that operate in relation to social classes, occupations or religious denomina-tions and that makes jokes about these groups possible.

The question that remains is: why are the Belgians, Irish, Poles, Pontians, etc. singled out as the butts of jokes about stupidity? It is possible, of course, that some of these peoples really are stupid and that the jokes are a mere matter of observation.[6] However, I think it unlikely that this is the case. Similarly, there is not much mileage in the view that the joke-tellers somehow collectively select the butts of their jokes about stupidity by picking on a group they particularly dislike or feel threatened by.[7] It is true that, other things being equal, people do enjoy jokes more if they are at the expense of groups they dislike; but other things are rarely equal. A cursory examina-tion of Table 1 reveals: (a) that there is a very wide range of sentiments held by the joke-tellers about their butts; and (b) that the butts of the jokes are not the groups whom the joke-tellers are likely to dislike most. In almost every case the joke-tellers have fought a major war that has threatened their very national existence with a people *other* than the butts of their jokes.[8] Yet it is *not* these groups who are the subject of jokes about stupidity.

In a fit of sly desperation, the upholders of the jokes-are-an-index-of-conflict-and-hostility theory are apt to claim that somehow the hostility and jokes have been displaced, rather like a sort of collective slipped disc. On this view Americans tell jokes about the Poles to 'take the heat off the Blacks' and En-glishmen tell jokes about the Irish because it would be 'dreadful-ly bad form' to engage in jocular Paki-bashing.[9] There are many objections to this thesis, quite apart from the fact that it is apparently the ultimate in untestable and infinitely elastic rubber theories. After all, Americans, *do* tell jokes about Blacks and Hispanics, Englishmen about Jamaicans and Pakistanis, Germans about Turks, and Frenchmen about North Africans; and the jokes appear much more negative and critical than do the jokes about the Poles, the Irish or the Belgians. It is precise-ly for this reason that such jokes are not generally told in public. The censorship of the cruder jokes about Blacks or sex from radio and television is merely an indication of who holds bureaucratic power in society; it is not a statement about widely held patterns of informal rules about joke-telling.[10]

The Irish/Polish/Belgian jokes are not in any sense a substitute for cruder, racist jokes; rather they are an entirely different genre of jokes that have evolved in response to a quite different kind of social situation. The key to an understanding of the nature of this social situation and its link with the standard stupidity script is systematic comparison. What do the butts of 'Irish jokes' listed in Table 1 have in common, both in their objective social circumstances and in the nature of their relationship with the joke-tellers? The first thing to note is how very similar they are to those who tell the jokes about them. For the joke-tellers, the butts are the closest and most familiar of neighbours, the most remote and provincial of their own people, or long-established and half-assimilated minorities. In general their relationship may be described as one of centre to periphery. The centre laughs at the alleged stupidity of the periphery, at people who are seen not as aliens but rather as comic versions of themselves, at people who are not fearful and incomprehensible but the comic shapes of the self seen in a gallery of distorting mirrors.[11]

The nature of this centre-periphery relationship may be geographical, cultural, linguistic, economic, or any combination of all four. The butts of 'Irish jokes' tend to live on an offshore island (Newfoundland, Tasmania, Ireland), on a remote coast facing nowhere (Kerry, Ostfriesland, Trebizond), on a distant peninsula (Yucatan, southern Italy), or in a remote border area (Kurdistan, Rasht, Nubia, Narino, Karelia). These areas are all far from the main centres of population and trade routes. Partly in consequence, they tend also to be less economically developed and more reliant on agriculture or fishing than the metropolitan centre where the joke-tellers live. The ethnic stupidity script is thus a version of the age-old comic stupidity script about country bumpkins, rubes, rustics, clodhoppers, rednecks, peasants, hicks, backwoodsmen, hill-billies, hayseeds, swedes or wurzels. The migration of labour tends to be from this rural periphery to the heavy industries of the centre, providing unskilled labourers for the building and construction industry and, in the past (and even today in semi-industrial countries), the lowest rank of domestic servants. Often poor peasants leaving the land have gone even further afield: the Irish to America, Australia and New Zealand; the Portuguese to Brazil (and incidentally to San Francisco); the Poles to Pennsylvania, Buffalo, Detroit, Chicago; and the Ukrainians to Canada.[12] In each case, such people have become the butts of ethnic jokes about stupidity told by those already occupying the skilled and managerial positions in industry. This theme is particularly strong in American jokes about Poles and British jokes about the Irish. Thus:

> 'What is the first thing a proud Polish father buys for his baby son? Booties with cleats.'

> 'How do you confuse an Irishman?
> Give him two shovels and tell him to take his pick.'

> 'Who was the Welsh king of Poland?
> John L. Lewis.'[13]

> 'How do you tell an Irish solicitor?
> Charcoal-grey donkey jacket and highly polished wellies.'

> 'A Sop was working on a building site in America when he fell from the fourth storey but got up unhurt. A circus proprietor heard about this and went to offer him a job. "Do you think you could jump off the tenth storey safely," he asked him. "Of course he could," said the foreman, "provided he landed on his head."'[14]

> 'The Irish attempt to climb Mt Everest has failed. They ran out of scaffolding.'

Gradually, of course, the new arrivals from the periphery, or their descendants, are upwardly mobile into skilled and responsible occupations. In the United States, the Poles replaced the Irish in jokes about proletarian stupidity because they arrived later and possessed even fewer relevant skills, thus quickly ending up at the bottom of the industrial system. In Britain, by contrast, earlier generations of Irish assimilated and became invisible; but there has never been any barrier to further Irish migration, as there was in the United States, with

the result that the population of 'greenhorns' has been maintained at a fairly steady level.[15]

In America upward mobility among the Irish was through
local politics; Irishmen gained control of city hall and employed
their compatriots as contractors or policemen.[16] Wherever the
initial move up the ladder is achieved through politics rather
than business or education, the comic stupidity tag takes the
form of jokes about stupidity *in power*. The butts of such jokes,
like aristocrats or East European party bosses, lack 'merit', for
they have not achieved their position in open competition but by
creating or exploiting a local or national monopoly. The Irish-
Americans, the Afrikaners, the Hausa, the Italian southerners
and many others have been on the receiving end of jokes about
stupidity in power. Thus:

> *'A Hausa politician was asked what mineral resources his
> state had. "We have plenty of minerals," he replied. "We have
> Coca Cola, we have Fanta, we have Sprite."'*

> *'Van der Merwe was put in charge of a new integrated tourist
> bus taking foreign visitors round Pretoria. He assembled his
> multinational group of customers and told them, "I know you
> all think everything is segregated by colour in South Africa
> but it isn't true on my bus. As far as I am concerned you can
> all be green. Right then, everybody on board, light green at
> the front, dark green at the back"'*

> *'Motor cycle cop: "Where's your third party?" Van der Merwe:
> "Hell, I'm from the Orange Free State. We don't even have a
> second party."'*

In a similar way we find the stupidity script being applied to
the dumb Irish-American or Afrikaner cop, to the southern
recruited *carabinieri* in Italy, to the unskilled rustics who fill
the militia of Poland or Czechoslovakia; all of whom are or were
essentially meritless political appointees.[17] In such jokes, those
exercising authority are mocked as dumber than those whom
they police:

> *'Doyle, who had just joined the cops in Baltimore, was told by
> the sergeant: "Your beat is from here to that red light in the*

*distance." Doyle vanished and only turned up a week later in*
*a state of exhaustion. "Where the hell have you been," said the*
*sergeant. "Well," said Doyle, "that red light was on the back*
*of a truck."* [18]

The monopoly/competition dichotomy is as important for the
formation of stupidity scripts as the centre–periphery one.
Groups from the periphery who, through business acumen or
intellectual skill, succeed in the free competition of the market-
place or the examination hall, become the subjects of *canny
scripts*. This has been true of the Scots, Jews, Gabrovonians,
Milanese, Levantini, Regiomontanos, Paisas, Armenians, Gu-
jaratis, New England Yankees, Dutch, Swabians, Auvergnats,
Cardis.[19] Take the following example:

*'What do you call a Patel who doesn't run a (British) post-
office?*
*Doctor.'*

This is the very antithesis of the stupidity script, and it is
rooted in very fundamental differences in values, culture and
history. Ethnic success through politics is about the capture and
use of the monopoly power of the state to exclude competition, to
extract revenue and to dispense patronage; and this is in
marked contrast to the competitive individualism of the 'canny'.
There is a further non-material dimension of the centre–
periphery relationship which is rooted in language and culture.
It is often correlated with the material factors but can exist
independently. Belgium is at the very centre of the European
economy, but its people are at the edge of both the French- and
the Dutch-speaking worlds. The Walloons and the people of
Brussels take their language and culture from France and especially Paris, and *not* the other way round. The Dutch laugh at
the Flemings for speaking 'old-fashioned' Dutch, but the Flemish are in no position to reply.[20]
It is the people at the centre who are the arbiters of language
and culture. Their dominance is acknowledged at the periphery
(albeit with some ambivalence), and it is built into the local
status system. Thus the upper middle class of Dublin teach
their children to imitate the more prestigious forms of British

Table 2 *Language and ethnic jokes about stupidity*

| Country where jokes told about 'allegedly' stupid groups | Language of joketellers | Group alleged to be stupid in jokes | Language or languages spoken by the butt of the jokes | Nature of the relationship between the language of joke-tellers and that of their butts |
|---|---|---|---|---|
| Britain | English | Irish | English | 'Same' language spoken. The butts of the jokes who may live in the same or in an adjoining country speak a distinctive and 'provincial' version of the joke-tellers' language |
| France | French | French Swiss (Ouin-Ouin) | French | |
| | | Belgians | Walloon/French | |
| Netherlands | Dutch | Belgians | Flemish/Dutch | |
| Germany | German | Ostfrieslanders | Low German | |
| Greece | Greek | Pontians (Black Sea Greeks) | ('Archaic') Greek | |
| Italy | Italian | Southerners | Italian dialects | 'Same' language spoken. The butts of the jokes who may live in the same or in an adjoining country speak a distinctive and 'provincial' version of the joke-tellers' language |
| Canada (Ontario) | English | Newfies (Newfoundlanders) | English | |
| Egypt | Arabic | Si'Aidi (Southerners) | Arabic | |
| Denmark | Danish | Jutes of Aarhus | Danish | |
| Turkey | Turkish | Laz | Turkish | |
| Ireland | English | Kerrymen | English | |
| Austria | German | Burgenlanders | German (Hungarian influence) | The butt of the joke is a group on a linguistic boundary speaking a version of the joke-tellers' language that shows foreign influence |
| | | Carinthians | German (Slovene influence) | |
| Finland | Finnish | Karelians | Finnish (Russian influence) | |

| Country | Main language of society | Butt of jokes | Language of butt | Description |
|---|---|---|---|---|
| Mexico | Spanish | Yucatecos | (a) Maya (b) Spanish | The butt of the jokes is a linguistic minority on the periphery whose members may have only a limited knowledge of the main language of the society |
| Iran | Persian (Farsi) | Rashtis | (a) Turkish (b) Persian | |
| Iraq | Arabic | Kurds | (a) Kurdish (b) Arabic | |
| South Africa | (a) English (main) (b) Afrikaans | Afrikaners (Van der Merwe) | (a) Afrikaans (main) (b) English | The butts of the jokes are in an official bilingual country. They are in a majority in their own country or area but the joke-tellers' language has a stronger external base |
| Sweden | Swedish (only) | Finns | (a) Finnish (main) (b) Swedish | Finland is officially bilingual and so is South Africa |
| Sweden | Swedish | Norwegians | Norwegian | The butts of the jokes live in an adjoining country and speak a closely related language that is largely intelligible to the joke-tellers |
| Denmark | Danish | Norwegians | Norwegian | |
| Spain | Spanish | Portuguese | Portuguese | |
| Australia | English | Irish | English | The butts of the jokes are immigrants or descendants of immigrants who already spoke a version of the main language of their new country |
| New Zealand | English | Irish | English | |
| Brazil | Portuguese | Poles (and locally Italians, Portuguese, etc.) | Portuguese | |
| United States | English | Poles (and locally Italians, Portuguese, etc.) | English | The butts of the jokes are immigrants or the descendants of immigrants who originally spoke a different language but have learned the main language of their new country |
| Canada (west) | English | Ukrainians | English | |

English, and make fun of the more distinctively Irish speech of the Kerrymen: 'What is social mobility? A Kerryman with a Cork accent.'[21] Similarly, the educated Francophones of Brussels strive to eliminate Belgicisms – traces of Bruxellois and odd fragments of Flemish – from their speech and imitate the usages of Paris.[22] There are many similar and also subtly different language relations that lead to jokes, as we can see from Table 2.[23]

Clearly, there are a number of patterns of linguistic dominance illustrated in Table 2. However, the general effect is often the same. The butts of the jokes feel that the language belongs as of right to the joke-tellers, and that they are involved in an unequal competition on someone else's linguistic territory. What is more, the butts of the jokes feel that their disadvantaged linguistic situation is not a symmetrical or reversible one. Speakers of major languages such as English, French and German may be ridiculed while in one another's countries for speaking the local language badly. However, each knows that they have a powerful linguistic base of their own to which they can retire and where it is *they* who will dominate. Peoples on a linguistic periphery do not and cannot feel such confidence, for their own speech is either (a) not a separate language but merely a 'funny' version of the joke-tellers' own, or (b) the weak and irrelevant half of a bilingual situation; as, for instance, where they have to learn the joke-tellers' language because it is culturally or economically valuable to them, but the joke-tellers need never bother to learn theirs. The speakers of Celtic languages must learn English or French, but for the English or French there is no pay-off from learning Welsh, Breton, Erse, Manx or Cornish. Finns learn Swedish, both because it is one of the official languages of their country (and in the past the main language of education and culture) and because Sweden is their bigger, richer, more culturally prestigious neighbour where many Finns migrate to seek employment. Swedes in Sweden, by contrast, have no reason to learn Finnish. Poles emigrating to the United States have to master English, but for Americans of non-Polish ethnic origin, there is no point in knowing Polish.[24]

The impact on a people of one-way linguistic dominance has been marvellously portrayed by James Joyce in his *Portrait of the Artist as a Young Man*. Stephen Dedalus has a minor confrontation with the Dean of his college, who is an English Jesuit:

[The Dean] thrust forward his under jaw and uttered a dry
short cough.
– To return to the lamp, he said, the feeding of it is also a
nice problem. You must choose the pure oil and you must be
careful when you pour it in not to overflow it, not to pour in
more than the funnel can hold.
– What funnel? asked Stephen
– The funnel through which you pour the oil into your lamp.
– That? said Stephen. Is that called a funnel! Is it not a
tundish?
– What is a tundish?
– That. The . . . the funnel.
– Is that called a tundish in Ireland? asked the dean. I never
heard the word in my life.
– It is called a tundish in Lower Drumcondra, said Stephen,
laughing, where they speak the best English.
– A tundish, said the dean reflectively. That is a most
interesting word. I must look that word up. Upon my word I
must.
His courtesy of manner rang a little false, and Stephen
looked at the English convert with the same eyes as the
elder brother in the parable may have turned on the
prodigal . . . The dean repeated the word yet again.
– Tundish! Well now, that is interesting!
– The question you asked me a moment ago seems to me
more interesting. What is that beauty which the artist
struggles to express from lumps of earth, said Stephen
coldly. The little word seemed to have turned a rapier point
of his sentiveness against this courteous and vigilant foe. He
felt with a smart of dejection that the man to whom he was
speaking was a countryman of Ben Jonson. He thought:
– The language in which we are speaking is his before it is
mine. How different are the words *home, Christ, ale, master*,
on his lips and on mine! I cannot speak or write these words
without unrest of spirit. His language, so familiar and so
foreign, will always be for me an acquired speech. I have not
made or accepted its words. My voice holds them at bay. My
soul frets in the shadow of his language.[25]

Stephen Dedalus feels his lack of knowledge of the word 'funnel' to be a mark of provincial ignorance, whereas the Dean's ignorance of its synonym 'tundish' (a word that Dedalus later discovers is, in fact, of English, not Irish, origin) merely provides the dean with an excuse for condescension. 'The Artist' used the English language with genius, whereas the dean lives on only in Joyce's portrayal; but it is not their relative individual talents nor even the dean's position of clerical and academic authority that determines the asymmetrical situation of the two men. Rather, it is the fact that the dean alone belonged to the group that possessed the dominant language. Dedalus's wry anger is that of a clever man temporarily trapped in a position of collectively defined stupidity. It is a common situation, and one which tends to ensure that the flow of jokes about stupidity is far greater in one direction than the other. When I asked a distinguished scholar from Finland, whose people are the butt of Swedish jokes about stupidity, why there was a relative lack of Finnish jokes about the Swedes (who to an outsider appear an infinitely more tedious people than any of those Scandinavian neighbours whom the Swedes so disdain), he replied:

> The Finns have special deep-ingrained hang-ups about their long subordination to the Swedish language and culture ... deep down many Finns still feel inferior to the Swedes and somehow it is not easy to make jokes in such a frame of mind. ... At one time there was a conscious attempt to spread jokes about the Swedes in Finland, but there was not much success.[26]

For the 85–90 per cent majority of Finns for whom Finnish is their first language (this despite the fact that Finland is officially bilingual), a visit to Sweden creates situations of condescension and inferiority that have to be managed and evaded. When I went from Helsinki to Uppsala in Sweden for an international conference in sociology in 1978, I met on the boat a Finnish colleague whom I knew well. I expressed pleasure at meeting someone who would be able to expedite our journey from the docks in Stockholm to Uppsala University because of his knowledge of the Swedish language. He laughed at my naïvety and said he was going to speak English alone in Sweden, because this was the only way he could meet the Swedes on terms of linguistic equality: 'My English is better than theirs, my Swedish isn't as good. If I speak English I'm just an anonymous foreigner; if I speak Swedish I'm a bloody Finn.'

It should be stressed that the Swedes are not as a nation in conflict with the Finns, who have not been under Swedish rule since 1814 when Finland was transferred to Russia. When the Soviet Union attacked Finland in 1940, and again during the continuation war 1941–44, many Swedes fought for Finland as volunteers; indeed, the great Finnish war leader Mannerheim was from Finland's Swedish minority. The issue is one of culture and language only. Similarly, the Swedes have not been in any conflict with the Norwegians since Norway seceded from Sweden before the First World War. None the less, the Swedes find the Norwegian attempts to create a national language extremely funny, and there have been many Swedish jokes about Ny-Norsk. The basis of the jokes, like Czech jokes about Slovaks, is that the other group's language is heard *not* as a separate incomprehensible tongue but rather as a 'funny' version of the joke-tellers' own language.

Many of the earliest British jokes about the Irish are language based. Notable among these is the famous Irish bull, where the speaker ends up making an internally contradictory statement due to an ignorant short-circuiting of the usual forms of English speech. J. O. Bartley has claimed that the Irish bull was a result of the persistence of literally translated Gaelic forms of expression in Irish English which did not fit easily with the usual English syntax and idioms.[27] There is also some indirect evidence in favour of Bartley's thesis from Wales and Scotland, where the English speakers tell jokes about the bulls perpetrated by their respective Celtic-speaking Highlanders.[28] Thus, for example:

*'During the controversy over the establishment of the Church of Wales the two chief protagonists were David Lloyd George and the Bishop of St Asaph. On one occasion Lloyd George addressed a meeting in a small Welsh village where he was introduced by one of the deacons of the local chapel as follows: "We all know the remarks made on this subject last*

*week by the Bishop of St Asaph who, in my opinion, is the
biggest liar in creation. Fortunately we have here tonight Mr
David Lloyd George who will be more than a match for
him.*"[29]

'*Donald Roy M'Vean when interrogated in regard to the
quality of his potato crop provided amuzement to the
Lowlanders around him by replying, "they are just fery goot
inteed, but fery seldom whatefer?"*'[30]

Many 'Irish' jokes of the twentieth century depend upon continued minor differences in usage or pronunciation between English English and Irish English, as in the following:

'*Is your father alive yet?
No, not yet.*'[31]

'*How to speak Irish in one easy lesson. Say very quickly:
WHALE
OIL
BEEF
HOOKED*'[32]

These jokes provide a curious backhanded tribute to the continued vitality of Irish English.[33] By contrast I know of only one American-Polish joke that incorporates a Polish word, expression or mode of speaking English:

'*Who was the Pole who invented the mini-skirt? Seymour
Dupa.*'[34]

This reflects the blunt fact that the Poles in America (like most immigrant groups) have *not* joined a multi-cultural society, nor even gone into the melting-pot; rather, they have been Americanized.[35] It is this that gives the lie to the kind of Polish joke told by the Slovak-American sociologist Michael Novak:

'*A Polish-American diplomat who had been stationed in
Warsaw returned to Virginia. At school his children were
called "Hunkies" and "dumb Polacks". Eventually one of
them retaliated and asked a young old-stock American, "Can
you speak Polish?" "No," was the reply. "Well then how does
it feel to be even dumber than a Polack?"*'[36]

It is a reasonable joke but it fails to make the point Novak wants since a knowledge of Polish is as irrelevant to the average American as a knowledge of Tibetan, Welsh, Guarani, Swahili or Afrikaans. Except for a few specialists, such knowledge is pointless, and an American not of Polish descent who struggled to master Polish would be regarded as stupid. There is a rather sad American joke that underlines this point:

*'Why do Poles learn English?*
*So they can read Joseph Conrad in the original.*[37]

It is for precisely this reason that Americans do not feel threatened by the Polish language in the way that they feel threatened by Spanish. (Spanish is threatening because of sheer numbers, America's border with Mexico and proximity to Latin America, and the linguistic belligerence of American Hispanics, whose language has a longer history in the New World than that of the US constitution.) The Poles, like nearly all the butts of the jokes listed, cannot pose a cultural threat to the dominant language. Rather the butts of ethnic jokes about stupidity are *transitional wavering peoples* whom we may call by the acronymn TWPs (the 'W' is pronounced like the 'oo' in took).[38] The TWPs are transitional and wavering in both space and time. As frontier peoples, they speak the language of the country but in a form that reveals the penetration of a neighbouring language. This may even produce jokes about phenomena such as the Wasserpolaks of Silesia, who lived on the frontiers of German, Polish and Czech speech and whose speech was seen as a hotchpotch of all three. Peoples of this kind blur the neat linguistic mental maps which people carry in their heads and in which national frontiers coincide with sharp language boundaries.[39] They constitute a comic zone of transition neither quite one thing nor another. The Swiss of Fribourg, a canton of mixed French and German speakers, are indeed laughed at for saying 'merci vielmal' for 'thank you very much'. The same problem afflicts immigrants, but in a framework of time instead of space. At first they are incomprehensible, but then they or their children learn to speak an (initially) faulty version of the local indigenous language.

These then are the *constant* factors that in greater or lesser

degree apply to all ethnic jokes about stupidity. However, there
are certain themes peculiar to jokes about the Irish, who for
instance are also caricatured as addicted to religion and to
alcohol. These alleged traits still form the basis of American
jokes about the Irish, even though the Poles, etc. have replaced
them in the stupidity jokes. There are two other points also
worth noting: the first is that it is *rare* for the British and the
French to tell jokes about the Irish or the Belgians being filthy,
whereas this is common in American and Canadian jokes about
Poles or Newfies. Thus we find jokes such as:

> *'Why won't they let Poles swim in Lake Michigan?*
> *Because they'd leave a rim.'*
>
> *'How do you get a Pole out of a swimming pool?*
> *Throw a bar of soap in.'*
>
> *'What is the most dangerous job in the Polish quarter of*
> *Chicago?*
> *Riding shot-gun on the garbage-truck.'*
>
> *'What is an example of air pollution?*
> *The Newfoundland parachute brigade.'*

The absence of such jokes in Britain is a further weak piece of
evidence that British stupidity jokes about the Irish are not
jokes of rejection. I say 'weak' because I think the main reasons
for this difference in patterns of transatlantic joking lies
elsewhere.[40]

The second point to note is that in many British jokes the Irish
are wits, not half-wits. This is quite rare, for most of the butts of
jokes about stupidity are seen as slow and heavy rather than
witty. However, the Irish have proved to be successful and witty
*users* of jokes about themselves, and British joke-lovers have
tacitly agreed to this.[41] Here are some examples:

> *'An Irishman and a Scotsman were lost in a forest and*
> *finally as it grew dark they discovered an old wooden hut*
> *with only a scrawny chicken inside that was too small to*
> *make a meal for both of them. So they agreed to cook it, then*
> *to go to sleep and in the morning the chicken would go to the*

*man who had had the most pleasant dream. Soon after first light they woke and the Scot said, "I had a wonderful dream last night. I dreamed the angels had come down to earth and carried me away with them right up into heaven. Now what could be a happier dream than that – where's my chicken?" "Oh," replied the Irishman, "When I saw you going up into heaven with the angels like that, I thought you wouldn't be needing the chicken, so I got up and ate it."* [42]

'*An Irishman went to look for work on a building site. The English foreman said to him, "You Paddies are often too stupid to work on a modern construction like this. I'll have to test your brains first before we take you on. Now tell me what is the difference between a girder and a joist." "Ah that's easy," replied the Irishman. "Goethe wrote Faust and Joyce wrote Ulysses."*'

In such jokes the Irish play with the relations of words and reality, and with the sounds and the literal and figurative meanings of words in ways that again break the rules of speech and thought, but which also show that the Irish are the *masters* of them. Which, as Humpty Dumpty said, is all. [43]

## Notes

1. Christie Davies. Ethnic jokes, moral values and social boundaries. *British Journal of Sociology*, **33**(3) (1982), 383–403.
2. Leonard Feinberg, *The Secret of Humor*. Amsterdam: Rodopi, 1978, pp. 2–9.
3. Katherine Briggs, *British Folktales and Legends*. St Albans: Granada, 1977, pp. 51–3; Vicomte de Colleville and Fritz de Zeppelin, *Contes grotesques du Danemark*. Paris: Chamuel, 1896, pp. 1–4; Thomas Fuller, *The History of the Worthies of England*, vol. II. 1811 (1662), p. 206; Vera Gašpariková, *Ostovtipné prébehyi veliké cigánstva a žarty*. Bratislava: Tatran, 1980; Ellas Mary Leather, *The Folk-lore of Herefordshire*. Hereford: Jakeman and Carver, 1912, p. 255; Joan Rockwell, *Evald Tang Kristensen*, Aalborg: Aalborg UP, 1982, p. 285; Pandit Shyama Shankara, *Wit and*

*Wisdom of India*. New York: Roerich, 1934; Alfred Stapleton, *All about the Merry Tales of Gotham*, Nottingham: Pearson, 1900, pp. 9–11, 38–9, 164–5; Stith Thompson, *The Folktale*. Berkeley: University of California, 1977, pp. 19, 188–94.

4. Victor Raskin, *Semantic Mechanisms of Humor*. Reidel: Boston, 1985.

5. Larry Sloan, *The World's Worst Moron Jokes*. Los Angeles: Price/Stern/Sloan, 1975.

6. Richard Lynn, The social ecology of intelligence in the British Isles. *British Journal of Clinical Psychology*, **18** (1979), 1–12; Richard Lynn, The social ecology of intelligence in the British Isles, France and Spain. In M. P. Morton *et al.* (eds), *Intelligence and Learning*, pp. 561–5. New York: Plenum, 1979. In all three cases the average intelligence scores of those people living on the geographical, economic and cultural periphery of the national or multinational unit studied are markedly lower than for those living at the centre.

7. This view is advanced without any valid independent supporting evidence by: Sandra McCosh, *Children's Humour*. London: Granada, 1976; and Roger L. Welsch, The American numskull tales: the Polack joke. *Western Folklore*, **26** (1967), 183–6.

8. During and after the Second World War there was intense hostility towards the Japanese in Australia, Britain, Canada and the United States, but there are no ethnic jokes about them.

9. See Bengt af Klintberg, Negervitsar. *Tradisjon*, **13** (1983) 23–45. The author is quoting but not necessarily endorsing this view.

10. Cruder jokes are not censored in all joke books. See, for example, Julius Alvin, *Totally Gross Jokes*. New York: Zebra/Kensington, 1983; and Jackie Climent-Galant, *Les 200 plus drôles histoires racistes de LUI*. Paris: Filipacchi, 1979.

11. See also Mina and André Guillois, *Histoires Belges et Méchantes*. Paris: Menges, 1979, p. 15.

12. Stanislav Andreski, *The Prospects of a Revolution in the USA*. London: Tom Stacey, 1973, p. 83; P. Fox, *The Poles in*

*America*. New York: Arno, 1970; Thomas Sowell, *Ethnic America: a history*. New York: Basic Books, 1981.

13. John L. Lewis was the head of the American mineworkers union and a very powerful labour unionist and politician. The joke is about the ethnic and social class position of the Poles as unskilled workers – it is the American equivalent of British jokes about the Irish doing pick and shovel jobs in their wellies. The joke probably originated in Pennsylvania where the unskilled mineworkers came from South Wales and the poor peasantry of Poland.

14. From Petko Ogoiiski, *Chequered Stories*. Sofia, 1975 [original in Bulgarian]. The Šopi (plural of Šop) are peasants who live in a rural area near to Sofia and provide the capital with a fair proportion of its labourers, tram-drivers and unskilled workers generally. It is possible that they are the descendants of the Pechenegs, an ethnically distinct group.

15. See M. H. Lyon, The role of the settlement area in British race relations. In G. A. Harrison and John Peel (eds), Biosocial aspects of race, *Journal of Biosocial Science*, Supplement no. 1 (1969), pp. 163–72 (p. 167), Eric J. Thompson, Patterns of migration. In G. A. Harrison and J. B. Gibson (eds), *Man in Urban Environments*, pp. 30, 42–3. London: OUP, 1976.

16. David Noel Doyle and Owen Dudley Edwards (eds), *America and Ireland: 1776–1976*. Westport, Connecticut: Greenwood, 1980.

17. See for instance Sir W. S. Gilbert, *The Savoy Operas*. London: Macmillan, 1983, and especially *Iolanthe*, Act II, pp. 231–7; Sebastian Grill, *Graf Bobby and Baron Mucki*. Munich, 1949; T. Koenderman, J. Langen and A. Viljoen, *Van der Merwe*. Hillbrow: Lorton, 1975; Michael Mann, The working class. *New Society*, 4 Nov. 1976, 240–3 (p. 240); Sandro Medici, *Barzellette sui Carabinieri*. Milan: Tiger, 1980.

18. See also Joe Laurie, Jr, Harry Hershfield and Senator Ed Ford, 1947, p. 80. *Cream of the Crop*.

19. Christie Davies, Jewish jokes, anti-semitic jokes and Hebredonian jokes. In Avner Ziv (ed.), *Jewish Humor*, pp. 75–98. Tel Aviv: Papyrus/University of Tel Aviv, 1986.

20. On Belgium see William Petersen, On the sub-nations of

Western Europe. In Nathan Glazer and Daniel P. Moynihan (eds), *Ethnicity, Theory and Experience*. Cambridge, Mass: Harvard UP, 1975.

21. Evidence congruent with this view, though not always directly to the point at issue, may be found in Diarmaid Ó Muirithe (ed.), *The English Language in Ireland*. Dublin: Radio Telefis Eireann and Mercier, 1977.

22. Joseph Hanse *et al.*, *Chasse aux Belgicismes*, Brussels: Charles Plisnier, 1971.

23. Christie Davies, Language, identity and ethnic jokes about stupidity. *International Journal of the Sociology of Language*, **65** (1987), 39–52.

24. Joshua A. Fishman, Einar Haugen *et al.*, *Language Loyalty in the United States*. The Hague: Mouton, 1966, pp. 9–10, 121–2.

25. James Joyce, *Portrait of the Artist as a Young Man*. London: Cape, 1968 (1916), pp. 192–4.

26. Lauri Lehtimaja, letter to the author.

27. J. O. Bartley, *Teague, Shenkin and Sawney*. Cork: Cork UP, 1954, pp. 86, 208. See also Alan Bliss, The emergence of modern English dialects in Ireland, pp. 7–36, pp. 13–19, and P. L. Henry, Anglo-Irish and its Irish background, pp. 26–36 in Ó Muirithe, op. cit.

28. See also Max K. Adler, *Welsh and Other Dying Languages in Europe: a socio-linguistic study*. Hamburg: Helmut Buske, 1977, pp. 39–40, 45, 60, 66.

29. See also G. G. Coulton, *Four-score years*, London: Readers Union, 1945.

30. R. Ford, 1901 *Thistledown*. Paisley: Alexander Gardner, 1901, pp. 158–9.

31. See also T. W. H. Crossland, *The Wild Irishman*. London: Werner Laurie, 1905, p. 137.

32. Whitelands Rag, London, Whitelands College Students' Union, n.p., 1985.

33. See Benedict Kiely, Dialect and literature, pp. 88–99 (pp. 94–5) and John Garvin, The Anglo-Irish idiom in the works of major Irish writers, pp. 100–14, in Ó Muirithe, op. cit.

34. William Clements, The types of the Polish joke. *Folklore Forum*, bibliographic and special series No. 3 (1973).

35. See Andreski, op. cit., p. 114 and Will Herburg, *Protestant,*

*Catholic, Jew*. Garden City New York: Doubleday, 1960, p. 21.

36. Michael Novak, The Sting of Polish Jokes. *Newsweek*, 12 Apr. 1976, p. 13.

37. Alan Dundes, A study of ethnic slurs, the Jew and the Polack in the United States. *Journal of American Folklore*, **84** (1971) 186–203 (p. 201).

38. See John Edwards, *More Talk Tidy*. Cambridge: Brown, 1986, p. 38.

39. See Anthony D. Smith, *The Ethnic Revival in the Modern World*. Cambridge. CUP, 1981, p. 45.

40. For an explanation see Christie Davies, *Jokes are about People*. Bloomington, Indiana: Indiana UP (forthcoming).

41. See Sheridan Gilley, English attitudes to the Irish in England 1789–1900. In Colin Holmes, *Immigrants and Minorities in British Society*, pp. 81–110 (pp. 82–3). London: Allen and Unwin, 1978.

42. See also W. H. Howe, *Everybody's Book of Irish Wit and Humour*. London: Saxon, 1890, p. 162.

43. Lewis Carroll, *Through the Looking Glass and What Alice Found There*. In *The Works of Lewis Carroll*, p. 174. Feltham: Spring/Hamlyn, 1965 (1871).

# Chapter 5

# What's the joke? A look at children's humour

## Nicholas Tucker

Infants are born with a capacity to be amused and adults often get enormous pleasure from seeing children enjoy themselves. We also relish laughing at the young, as legions of pre-war collections on the lines of *The Amusing Sayings of Children* once brought out by Lady Cynthia Asquith can testify.

> Child: *'I don't like Mrs Brown.'*
> Mother: *'Why not?'*
> Child: *'For a reason.'*
> Mother: *'And what might that be?'*
> Child: *'Mrs Brown is the reason.'*[1]

But laughing with rather than at children is often a different matter. For one thing, even the nicest infant can be appallingly blunt, chuckling with disbelief on first meeting an adult midget, convulsed by the sound of stammering and helpless when confronted by red noses, large ears or projecting teeth. Some of their verbal comments can also be painfully embarrassing, as many a former *Punch* cartoon confirms.

*Child: 'What meat are we eating?'*
*Mother, turning away from venerable guest for a moment:*
*'Beef, dear.'*
*Child: 'But you said we were having Old Mutton-head for*
*lunch today!'[2]*

Accordingly a child soon has to learn when he or she can speak their mind or generally laugh out loud in public and when it is better to keep quiet. In this way infants are always liable to be scolded for laughing in the wrong place; at other times they may be helped by more positive means. Many children's books, for example, both amuse children and also provide excellent guidance as to what can safely be laughed at. Humour of the type most adults disapprove of is largely ignored in this literature, or else figures more by accident than design.

Nursery rhymes, for example, delight small children with the humour of language itself. Rhyme, reduplicated words (Humpty Dumpty) and catchy rhythms can always captivate a child, both when he or she comes across such devices in literature and when they try them out on themselves or each other. In Ruth Weir's study *Language in the Crib* many examples are quoted of the spontaneous rhyming and rhythm-making infants get up to when babbling to themselves before going to sleep, often laughing at their own inventions in the process. Later on rhymes about other people's names, whether original or not ('Mary, Mary, quite contrary'; 'Dan, Dan, the dirty old man') will give pleasure to all but the victims on the receiving end. Alliteration is also popular by way of verbal humour: and this is one reason for the appeal of the best-selling American children's author Dr Suess, one of whose books is named *Horton Hears a Who* and whose songs contain lines like 'Fifteen pickles and a purple plum'.[3]

The sheer sound of language often seems more attractive to children than its particular sense. While no one to this day is sure what the nursery rhyme 'Pop goes the weasel!' refers to, children simply like the sound it makes. Irritated at this occasional pleasure in the absurd, various critics over the centuries have tried rewriting certain nursery rhymes, but never to any effect. A nineteenth-century American writer of improving books for children named Samuel Goodrich went further by composing the following meaningless nursery rhyme on the spur of the moment, just to demonstrate how silly the whole genre was:

> Higglety, pigglety, pop!
> The dog has eaten the mop;
> The pig's in a hurry,
> The cat's in a flurry,
> Higglety, pigglety, pop!

But as Iona and Peter Opie, the magisterial compilers of *The Oxford Dictionary of Nursery Rhymes* point out, 'Because, in spite of everything, he was a bit of a genius Goodrich had unwillingly added to the store of nursery rhymes literature.'[4] For Goodrich's rhyme still crops up in anthologies today and was recently the subject of a children's opera by Oliver Knussen. By contrast, all his serious work for children is now forgotten.

Another form of humour children enjoy involves the incongruity of unexpected results in familiar circumstances. Early on babies will often protest loudly when parents adopt new hairstyles or else suddenly appear minus apparently permanent features such as a pair of spectacles. Later on such mild disguise or general dressing up can amuse a child no end once he or she is so sure of their environment that any temporary variation to it does not come over as a threat. In the same way, slapstick humour involving collapsing cars or disintegrating bicycles is funnier once it is appreciated how solid such objects can generally be expected to be. As with the game of peekaboo played all over the world, a child enjoys situations where the expected does not always happen so long as he or she feels reasonably secure in the first place. For a child with an abnormal dread of any sort of parental separation, peekaboo or hide-and-seek can be quite alarming. But most children take these various diversions in their stride, welcoming the chance to experiment with their growing ability to control the mild anxiety common to such games. A literary variant on this type of humour is found in suspense rhymes like 'Rock-a-bye, baby', with that agonizing wait each time for the sudden fall at 'Down will come baby, cradle and all!'

Different humour of the unexpected arises from people who look or behave in marked contrast to the norm. A child or adult

physically different from everyone else can usually be sure of
intense curiosity from infants, however dismayed parents may
sometimes be by such responses outside the circus, film or pantomime. Faced by this insensitivity, adults have the delicate
task of discouraging its public appearance while pandering to it
when directed against grotesque imaginary characters such as
Billy Bunter. Once more, there is an element of anxiety here,
given that these risible characters trigger off children's fears
that they too might one day become the butt of others' mockery.
Laughter here may not only relieve anxiety but also protect the
individual from feeling pity at the contemplation of another
person's misfortunes. Thus the savagery of this type of humour,
with fat children always the cause of more jokes among others
than they ever dare articulate on their own, and spastic children
often the butts of unpleasant 'black' humour. As Konrad Lorenz
has pointed out, 'Laughter produces simultaneously a strong
fellow feeling among participants and joint aggressiveness towards outsiders.' It follows that another of a child's earliest
concerns is to make sure he or she is not going to be one of those
outsiders, even if this means re-routing malicious humour in
the direction of others more vulnerable than themselves. If this
outsider happens to be an ineffective teacher, so much the better. As poor Mr Mell once pleaded while being hounded by
Steerforth and other little horrors from David Copperfield's
early education, 'What does this mean? It's impossible to bear.
It's maddening. How can you do it to me, boys?' But alas, they
could, and did, and still will, given the chance.

In fact as children get older the aggressive content of their
humour becomes more pronounced. As infants they could occasionally get away with furious tantrums but as schoolchildren
'old enough to know better' they are expected to obey more rules,
especially those concerning self-control. Perhaps this is why the
knock-about humour of comic strip and cartoon film becomes
popular around now, involving as it does characters who still
behave with an infant's emotional lability. Much of this aggression is directed by the small and weak against the strong and
powerful in stories where bullies are thwarted, policemen
cheeked, fierce schoolteachers disobeyed and parents ridiculed;
all a very satisfying fantasy alternative for what most children
are too scared to do in real life. Classics of humour like *The Wind*

*in the Willows* also embody these anti-authority themes, with Toad the children's Falstaff, forever breaking conventional rules and almost getting away with it. In *Alice's Adventures in Wonderland*, adult characters are made to seem more childish than Alice herself, and the Christopher Robin series poke fun both at adults (Eeyore and Owl) and at children themselves (Pooh and Piglet). While adult characters usually reassert their control by the end of such stories, this is not necessarily an unpleasant coming down to earth for young readers. Restoring the social status quo each time after a short period of anarchy means that children can fully enjoy running amok in their imagination without ever worrying that such behaviour could eventually lead to the frightening destruction of the everyday security they also like to take for granted in fiction as well as in real life.

While all this humour makes excellent psychological sense to the child, it is usually only allowed fullest expression either when adults are out of the way or else when aimed at the pretend rather than the real. Here jokey music in films, grotesque drawings in comic strip, clowns' make-up in the circus and a profusion of exclamation marks plus amusing pictures in books all indicate to the child where laughter is expected and permissible. Parents probably suspect that among each other children still make jokes that can be cruel and tasteless about human targets such as vulnerable class-mates or members of a particular ethnic group. But so long as they keep quiet about such topics in adult company and gradually learn to recognize the cues distinguishing between, say, the comic view of aggression in Laurel and Hardy films and a serious view of the same thing in TV news items about actual warfare, then each generation can happily enjoy the humour of the other.

The only time this process of adult assimilation often falters is in the area of lavatorial and sexual humour, both favourite sources for children's jokes. There is no mystery as to why these particular aspects to life should stimulate such abundant humour both for children and of course for many adults too, though seldom at the same time and place. Where children are concerned, scatological and sexual humour operate as useful safety-values for expressing the aggression, anxiety and thwarted exhibitionism consequent upon the banning of various taboo practices and behaviour popular with infants but increasingly frowned on by the adults in charge. What makes this humour different later on is the way adults often refuse to recognize its right to exist, even though they both enjoyed similar jokes when young themselves and frequently continue to do so, in modified forms, in their maturity. So while children can expect to find reflections of the rest of their humour in books, films and adult jokes, albeit in a generally gentler form, lavatorial and sexual humour is met either by disapproving silence or else by sharp words and the occasional smack.

Such has not always been the case. Early nursery rhymes were not infrequently lavatorial or sexual in subject-matter, with the versions we know now often a triumph of nineteenth-century bowdlerization. The same is true of various traditional folk-songs, with 'Oh, no John!' once far more explicit about what exactly was being refused than is evident from its cleaned-up text today. As for fairy stories, it is not so long ago that Sleeping Beauty was woken up by amatory behaviour on the part of the young prince considerably more emphatic than a mere opening kiss. *The Arabian Nights Entertainments* too were originally far spicier until finally reissued by Andrew Lang in 1898, 'With the omission of pieces suitable for Arabs and old gentlemen'.

Within families, there is often a certain tolerance of various 'rude' words and jokes so long as everyone closes ranks when visitors appear or else once outside the home. This public prudery reflects the growing expectations of lavatorial and sexual privacy found in Britain over the last two centuries. Why this should have occurred is something of a mystery, with some historians linking it with the drift away from the countryside and its natural exposure to, and interest in, animal body products and sexuality. But whatever the cause, children today are soon faced by apparently arbitrary adult reactions to some of their favourite topics for humour, rather as nineteenth-century agricultural workers would find themselves scolded by folklorists such as the Reverend Sabine Gould about their choice of traditional erotic folk-songs cheerfully sung by generations before.

The consequence of such adverse reactions can be far-reaching. Adults who deny the existence of children's grosser forms of humour help preserve an idealized image of childhood that is still a hangover from Victorian sentimentality. Children who clearly do not measure up to such an ideal, and this means most of them, will be made to feel unnaturally dirty-minded, making civilized discussion about sexuality between the generations extremely difficult. So when it becomes important for children to raise these matters with parents or teachers, as for example in cases of sexual abuse, they may be too embarrassed or shamefaced to do so. As it is, the relevant vocabulary available to them will tend to be that of the coarse joke or playground chant for want of any more acceptable phraseology, given that sex education in Britain lags behind standards of frankness and early understanding set, for example, in Sweden. Sexual molesters, used already to relying upon their victim's shamed silence, can only benefit from a system that encourages children to feel guilty about all matters of sexuality, even on those occasions when they are victims of older people.

The same wall of silence affects other ways in which we think about children today. Books written about childhood remain generally coy about the lavatorial and sexual interests of the young, with hardly any mention of these areas in Iona and Peter Opie's otherwise comprehensive study *The Lore and Language of Schoolchildren*.[5] Jean Piaget, the greatest twentieth-century psychologist, also steered his researches well away from such topics when questioning infants about their various beliefs and attitudes. Such caution may have been inevitable, since asking children about their sexual interests could be conceived of as a type of indecent assault in itself, helping to explain the paucity of such research in current literature. At the same time books written for children also studiously avoid any mention of taboo areas; the only times most of them sound anything like normal playground conversation are inadvertent. One recalls A. A. Milne's poem in *The House of Pooh*, with its unconsciously ambiguous line 'Pooh is simply poohing like a bird.'[6] A more extraordinary moment crops up in one of Richmal Crompton's best-selling books about her famous mischievous boy hero William. In a story entitled 'Aunt Jane's treat' from *William the Fourth* (1924), the author describes how one of William's respectable maiden aunts accompanies him to a fair. Once there the excitement of the occasion overcomes her and she finally takes a ride on a merry-go-round, mounting – as the author puts it – 'A giant cock. It began. She clung on for dear life. It went faster and faster. There came a gleam into her eyes, a smile of rapture to her lips. . . . She seemed to find the circular motion anything but monotonous. It seemed to give her a joy that all her blameless life had so far failed to produce.'[7]

That children's literature only contains such passages by accident is one more indication of the sentimental image of childhood adults prefer to maintain and also attempt to foist on children themselves. Not surprisingly children often reject such literature later on for its obvious distortions of what childhood is really like. Those few children's authors who are beginning to write more frankly have been considerably criticized, with Richard Adams receiving more letters of protest about the phrase 'Piss off!' in Watership Down than he has over any other aspect of his fine novel.[8] Raymond Briggs's earthy picture-book Fungus the Bogeyman also had an uneasy reception on first publication,[9] and Roald Dahl's uninhibited humour still puts him out of favour with some critics whatever his popularity with the young. Writers for older children like Judy Blume have also become unpopular in some circles for their occasionally more sexually explicit passages.

Talking honestly to children by way of contrast is not always easy whether we are discussing either them or ourselves, and no one is suggesting that every inhibition should disappear where the public airing of children's sexual interest is concerned. But leaving nearly all such discussion of sexuality to the hurly-burly of the playground instead is to let children and their most typically vulgar jokes do some of our apparently dirty work for us while we stay on the edge trying not to hear what is going on. The fact that we too once chanted the same blue rhymes and songs that we now pretend to be so shocked about is perhaps the biggest joke of the lot, but not necessarily a very healthy one.

### Notes

1. Quoted in Jane Waller, Some Things for the Children. London: Duckworth, 1974.
2. Ruth Weir, Language in the Crib. The Hague: Mouton & Co., 1962.

3. Dr Seuss, *Horton Hears a Who*. New York: Random House, 1954.
4. Iona and Peter Opie, *The Oxford Dictionary of Nursery Rhymes*. London: Oxford University Press, 1951.
5. Iona and Peter Opie, *The Lore and Language of Schoolchildren*. London: Oxford University Press, 1959.
6. A. A. Milne, *The House at Pooh Corner*. London: Methuen, 1928.
7. Richmal Crompton, *William the Fourth*. London: George Newnes, 1924.
8. Richard Adams, *Watership Down*. London: Rex Collinge, 1973.
9. Raymond Briggs, *Fungus the Bogeyman*. London: Hamish Hamilton, 1982.

# Chapter 6
# Political cartooning

## Nicholas Garland

There are a number of questions that all cartoonists are asked about their work: How do you get your ideas? Are some people more difficult to draw than others? Does your editor censor what you do? How long does it take to draw a cartoon? Even, what else do you do? – as if knocking off light-hearted sketches could not occupy a grown man for very long. The question I asked *myself* when I came to write this chapter was: Why is it that political cartoons, these empheral, inevitably quickly conceived and executed comic drawings, are so highly valued by newspaper editors and readers? Part of the answer, I am sure, lies in the tradition (here in Britain at least) that the views of the cartoonist may differ widely from those expressed more formally elsewhere in the newspaper. From this particular freedom given to, or seized by, the cartoonist, whether or not it is used on a particular day, derives a large part of their strength. Politically, cartoons may be a safety valve undermining dogmas and pomposity as much in their own newspapers as in the world outside. Intellectually, they represent the freedom to play with ideas – to contradict oneself, to follow a thought to an absurd conclusion, to change one's mind.

In this chapter, I intend to pursue some of these questions by teasing apart the separate elements that make up a cartoon, and then looking at the process by which they are put together and fused into the finished product. In fact, political cartoons are not so much rapier thrusts (which they are often called) as they are missiles, which although quite small, carry at least three explosive warheads. First, caricature – the humorously or maliciously distorted representation of politicians; second, the actual political comment, criticism or stance communicated in the drawing; and third, the vehicle or image chosen to convey the political point. When brought together, at its best the effect is formidable. The *apparent joke* can contain a reverberating, subversive power.

First then, caricature. For everyone, there is a kind of magic involved in putting down lines on paper that give so vivid an impression of someone's actual presence, that for a second they might be in the room with you. As a child I carefully copied caricatures from newspapers and found to my utter delight that by borrowing the devices of another artist I could work the spell myself. The reduction of a familiar human being – a schoolmaster perhaps, or a politician, or a film star – to a comical little drawing fascinated me. I was well aware, even then, that by creating this form of likeness, I had stolen something from an individual and in an odd way gained a kind of power over him.

We all have an image of ourselves that we try to maintain, and we work quite hard to get other people to believe in it too. Caricaturists work even harder directly against this effort. Even when exercised without any intention to wound, good caricature has the power to reduce the dignity, and therefore the authority, of those represented. Just as it is always a bit of a shock unexpectedly to catch sight of oneself reflected in a shop window or wandering moronically across a TV security screen, so it is disturbing to see oneself caricatured. In just the same way no one likes to be mimicked, which is why we reach for mimicry in the course of rows: 'No I didn't', 'Yes you did', to create three-dimensional verbal caricatures intended to sting.

How does a caricature become established? Caricatures are not static; they grow and evolve in the cartoonist's work, taking the readers with them. When a new political figure takes his or her place on the stage the cartoonists first of all carefully produce fairly academically accurate likenesses of the newcomer. Gradually, certain features become established as standing for the individual. Mr Kinnock's freckles, for example, or Mrs

Thatcher's bouffant hair and pointy nose, or Mr Heath's wide smile. The fact that when you meet Mr Heath you notice that his mouth is rather small and pursed, or that Mrs Thatcher's hair is no longer all fluffed out, is neither here nor there. They have been reinvented by the cartoonist and are perfectly recognizable in their transmogrified form. Of course, politicians do not really begin to look like the cartoons we draw of them. What happens is that we create a kind of distorting glass through which they are seen.

Sometimes an individual makes this process very easy. General de Gaulle's great height was a gift to cartoonists, as are Mr Healey's bushy eyebrows. Sometimes politicians craftily invent props such as umbrellas, pipes, bow-ties, eccentric hair-styles and moustaches, and very grateful we are too.

In the process of developing one of these hieroglyphs, I study the work of other cartoonists very closely. Vicky, the famous left-wing cartoonist who worked for Lord Beaverbrook for many years, always said he got pretty irritated when he saw another artist making use of solutions that had cost him much labour to invent. I frankly long for the day when I see that I have influenced someone in this way and would like to take this opportunity of gratefully thanking Vicky's shade for the thousands of times I have made use of his powers of observation. In fact, I consider him to be the greatest political cartoonist of this century. He was heavily influenced by David Low early in his career, but, like the wren launched from the back of a soaring eagle, in the end he flew a little higher.

In its directness and simplicity, caricature does not allow for fine degrees of criticism. It has an awful bluntness. It cannot dilute its message to say, for example: 'You are behaving like a fool.' It says more succinctly: 'You idiot!' It strikes at the most vulnerable and private side of its targets. Writers can elaborate clear distinctions between various aspects of a man's life, finding some much more attractive than others: so and so is an absolute swine to his colleagues but a devoted father and husband. Caricaturists cannot go in for such fine degrees of criticism even if they wish to. They pursue a different kind of truth.

Annibale Caracci, the Italian who in the sixteenth century first practised this subversive form of portraiture, observed:

Is not the caricaturist's task exactly the same as the
classical artist's? Both see the lasting truth beneath the
surface of mere outward appearance. Both try to help nature
successfully accomplish its plan. The one may strive to
visualize the perfect form and to realize it in his work; the
other to grasp the perfect deformity, and *thus* reveal the
very essence of a personality. A good caricature, like every
other work of art, is more true to life than reality itself.

The truth that caricature reaches for has, I think, to do with the
transitory nature of all political power and the vulnerability of
even the most mighty. Caricatures can therefore even be oddly
comforting as well as very funny. A monster such as Hitler or
Stalin is suddenly less terrifying; fear, anxiety and a sense of
paralysing hatred cannot easily coexist with laughter. I im-
agine this is why *Pravda* does not feature daily caricatures of
the members of the Russian governing class.

'The most perfect caricature', said Max Beerbohm, and he
should know, 'is that which, on a small surface, with the simplest means, most accurately exaggerates, to the highest point,
the peculiarities of a human being, at his most characteristic
moment, in the most beautiful manner.' The last phrase of that
charming definition is particularly important. A perfect caricature must be well drawn. Cartoonists sometimes seem to think
that the more grotesquely they distort a figure, the more meaning they pack into the drawing; or even that the more crudely
and violently they dash down their lines, the more devastating
the effect of their work. The opposite is true. Caracci's observation that the caricaturist's task is the same as the classical
artist's, that is, to 'see the lasting truth beneath the surface',
means that the cartoonist must take as much care as any classical artist over drawing, composition, tone and so on.

Caricature thus lies at the heart of political cartooning. From
their success in creating lively, vivid caricatures that begin to
develop an existence of their own, cartoonists derive much of
what power or influence they have. But there is more to it than
that. The characters form part of the dramatization of the idea
itself, the point the cartoon is making – the reason for its existence. The saying 'a drawing is worth a thousand words' is, of
course, extremely gratifying to cartoonists. Although a political

cartoon may contain only a very simple political notion easily
conveyed in half a dozen words, the bare statement of the idea
does not begin to do justice to the force of the cartoon. That
derives from the vehicle itself which, besides caricature, requires some or all of a mixture of caricature, metaphor, distor-
tion, surealism, deliberate misunderstanding and mockery.

First, a word about the ideas themselves. In some ways, and
with only a modest knowledge of political issues, the comment
or attitude underpinning the cartoon is the simplest part of the
whole. The cartoonist notices that the government is heading
for a showdown with the unions, or that the current East/West
talks are going frightfully well, or that, say, unemployment is
the main issue in a coming by-election. This much most of us can
do, and it is a necessary part of the creation of any political
cartoon; but it is not sufficient. The invention or discovery of a
scene or tableau that will convey and illuminate the political
point of a cartoon is the most difficult part of the process. I write
as though 'the idea' were somehow separate from the vehicle or
image that carries it, whereas of course they are inseparable.
(This is why I grind my teeth when I am asked 'Do you write the
captions as well as do the drawings?') Let me try to illustrate
what I mean.

Because politics are about an endless circular battle against
age-old problems, cartoons often feature politicians engaged in
some sort of contest. Boxing matches, horse-races and jousting
are all popular, and successive generations of ministers are
drawn fighting it out with inflation, unemployment, economic
crises, scandal and so on. But all kinds of other unlikely situations are devised to try to get across the complications of political reality. Cartoonists may cast their leaders in the role of
almost anything, from a guttering candle to a nuclear blast. The
point is that the choice of candle as opposed to nuclear blast *is*
the idea, an integral part of it: it says 'weak and providing little
illumination', as opposed to 'powerful and deadly'.

'Getting an idea' is finding the right vehicle for an opinion,
one which simultaneously expresses and illuminates it. On good
days an 'idea' pops up complete with cast, props, setting and, if
necessary, caption. It is as if someone had put a slide into a
projector, and in my mind's eye I study it and can make
appropriate changes. But although I have done this for twenty

years or so, at its heart it remains an essentially mysterious
process; each day I do not know whether it will work or not, or
how smoothly.

On a difficult day, the political thought has to be struggled
with in order to find the right image to convey it. It has to be
looked for, which involves a search for analogies. Let me give
some examples. Analogies for political dramas can be found in
famous events from history, literature or mythology. Some
events lodge in our minds because they vividly illustrate familiar human traits or predicaments. Thus a politician ignoring
the unhappy consequences of some act claps a telescope to a
blind eye. A minister dithering between several options will
appear as Hamlet gazing at an appropriately labelled skull.
Overweening ambition in one of our leaders may have him
flying too close to the sun, and plunging from the sky like Icarus.

It is an amusing game to list references of this sort that would
be instantly understood by any reasonably well-educated person. It would contain all of Alice in Wonderland; many Victorian paintings, such as *The Monarch of the Glen* and *Bubbles*;
certain famous posters ('Your Country needs You'; 'My Goodness My Guinness'); a great number of films and children's
books; and much of Kipling. In twenty years' time, of course, the
stock of common references may have changed altogether.
James Bond conveys more to my children than will Kipling.

Nursery rhymes are a particularly good source. You can practically see the cartoons forming in your mind's eye: 'Where are
you going to, my pretty maid?' 'Humpty Dumpty had a great
fall.' 'When the pie was opened, the birds began to sing.'
Shakespeare may always head the list, but the single line most
frequently quoted in this way is, I am sure: 'Please sir, I want
some more.'

Gradually, in the hunt for ideas of this kind, one learns to
engage in a process of highly deliberate wool-gathering. Let me
give you an example. When the Labour Party was walloped by
Mrs Thatcher in June 1983, I thought it would never recover.
Thoughts of death merged in my mind with the personality of
the elderly leader of the party. The fact that Michael Foot
carried a heavy responsibility for his party's plight was made
more poignant by his obviously profound love for the party. An
old man and a dying thing. An old man and his ailing child. A

*'I know when one is dead and when one lives;*
*She's dead as earth. – Lend me a looking glass*
*If that her breath will mist or stain the stone*
*Why then she lives.'* (King Lear)

dead daughter. King Lear speaking (see above):

I know when one is dead and when one lives;
She's dead as earth. Lend me a looking glass
If that her breath will mist or stain the stone
Why then she lives.

Lear, and perhaps even the audience, are unwilling for a moment to believe that Cordelia is quite dead. Was the Labour Party dead? Is this a real tragedy? Will not all the actors survive and stand before us taking their bow? The scene contains all these possibilities and expressed my own attitude pretty well; that is, 'The Labour Party has probably had it – but I hope not.'

Put together, all this means that the best, the most striking cartoons can be read at a glance. It probably requires that the idea contained in a political cartoon must not only be easily understood but even be already widely established *before* the cartoonist uses it. It could reasonably be argued that political cartoons are merely telling people what they already know in a highly simplified form.

Take David Low's wartime cartoons (see below). On the fall of France in 1940, Low did this drawing of a British Tommy standing on a rocky shore, shaking his fist at an advancing wave of Nazi bombers and crying out defiantly, 'Very well, alone.' Everyone who saw this cartoon on the day it was published already knew perfectly well that Britain now stood alone against a fearful enemy. Yet Low's representation of Britain's peril says infinitely more than a mere statement of the fact. There is something about the way the lightly armed soldier is shown standing his ground against the bombers, emerging like sinister little crosses from the black sky, which sets the mind

'VERY WELL, ALONE.'

racing through a hundred tales of undaunted heroes facing
dreadful odds. David slew Goliath; Horatius held the bridge;
Nelson ignored the signal ordering him back into line; bullies
*must* be stood up to sooner or later; the resonance of the cartoon
rolls on and on to this day.

The paradox is, therefore, that cartoons express very simple
ideas or attitudes through the use of a medium that allows them
to be extremely complex. In another example, Vicky summed up
his view of the nuclear deterrent in one witty drawing (see p.
84). He drew Duncan Sandys, then Minister of Defence, facing a
Russian bear. Clasping a revolver marked H-bomb to his own
temple, Sandys warns the bear, 'One step and I shoot!' Fantasy,
nonsense and preposterous over-simplification are cheerfully
jumbled up in this cartoon; but the bold statement of a truth we
already know comes through powerfully: if we use our nuclear
weapons, we die. But now just begin to consider the tangled
associations one has with a menacing bear. From Goldilocks
through to Daniel Boone, the way is long and intricate, yet all
that is the potential contained in Vicky's brilliant scratchy
lines; that, and, if we continue, much more. For what horrors the
image of a man blowing his own brains out sends shuddering
through our imaginations, and what anger is summoned up
from our unconscious against a suicide who is prepared to take
us with him?

In fact, there is also something outrageously unfair about this
cartoon, for in real life the whole point is that the bear too is
threatened with annihilation. We know that, and the Defence
Minister knows that; the cartoon raises the chilling question:
does the shambling bear know it? We do not often analyse
cartoons consciously in this way. But as we relish the joke and
take the point, the imagery works on us nevertheless. It is to
this unobtrusive density present in the best political cartoons
that I attribute their strength.

It took me a long time to realize this essential point about
political cartoons. They are not manifestos, and they are not in
any way suited to the presentation of subtle arguments. They
are fancies or free associations shared by the artist with the
readers. Just as the cartoonist may play, as it were, on the
unconscious mind of the reader, his own unconscious is also at
work. Recently, I did a drawing of Mr Kinnock on a visit to the

'One step, and I shoot!'

USA (see p. 86). I showed him to be very small, and surrounded by a forest of huge, striding legs. He was trying in vain to attract the attention of the towering, busy Americans by calling out in a friendly way: 'Hi there, fellers.... . Hiya, guys... .' I meant to show that the Americans were not all that interested in him; but a friend interpreted the cartoon back to me. He said, 'I liked your Reagan/Julius Caesar cartoon.' I did not know what he was talking about. He said, 'The one that showed Kinnock in the States – you know, 'We petty men walk under his huge legs, and peep about to find ourselves dishonourable graves.' I had not meant to express the view that the USA is a bit too big and influential, or the idea that Mr Kinnock, Cassius-like, was challenging the President's omnipotence. Yet that meaning was there too, and I was delighted to have it pointed out to me.

Thus, the problems that face cartoonists are concerned with, first, how to simplify the comment; and second, how to draw in a way that allows it to be freely associated to and enriched again. And as I have said, in a way these two problems are one, because the impact should be immediate and economical, able to be read and responded to in a flash. For this reason I never like editorial conferences about cartoons, and I never show roughs to my editors as some cartoonists do, because conferences and discussions tend to elaborate views and opinions instead of paring them down.

In the same way, when readers write in with suggestions for cartoons they are invariably too complicated. They say, 'I'd like to see a cartoon based on the famous game of bowls played by Sir Francis Drake at Plymouth. The bowls could be marked *unemployment, economic crisis* and *inner-city decay*; Drake could be shown as the Minister of Defence; he should have just thrown a bowl marked 'defence cuts' at his opponent, the Shadow Defence Minister, who is ...'; and so on. This would take a week to draw, take up a whole page and need an hour to read. This is what all my first efforts were actually like. It took me a long time to realize that my cartoons were not manifestos, and that they were not going to do very much to change anything. Luckily, around about this time, as I struggled each day to encapsulate short histories of the world in a space about four and a half inches deep across four columns, I was given some advice by

'HI THERE, FELLERS ... HIYA, GUYS ...'

Colin Welch, who was then deputy editor of the *Daily Telegraph* where I worked.

I cannot remember his exact words, but twenty years later the sense of what he said still guides every drawing I do. 'Your work is too earth-bound', he said. 'In the world created by cartoons there is no need to obey the rules of perspective, logic or gravity; no need to be historically accurate or consistent – absolutely anything can happen.' I felt I had been told to go out and play, and in the paradoxical way in which something may be achieved once you stop trying too hard to do it, I began to find cartooning easier. The notion that a cartoon might have a fantastical element to it – that it could be based on the logic of dreams, for example, and could even gain from it – at once began to affect the actual drawing. I saw that each representation of a politician did not have to be a portrait or even in any ordinary sense a likeness. Caricatures could be pared down; they could evolve into a sophisticated hieroglyph.

Herbert Morrison once asked Vicky, 'Why do you always draw me with such thin legs?' Vicky replied, 'To save ink.' In fact, the way to a good hieroglyph is hard. Artists frequently experience the frustration of being unable to recapture in a finished work the vigour and accuracy of the preparatory sketches. I always prefer the sketches in my note pad to the completed artwork. I know one artist who tried drawing his cartoons while travelling by train, in order to prevent his lines becoming too dead and correct. It did not work, the train swayed about too much. Unwilling to accept defeat, he experimented with drawing left-handed, but that proved too laborious. I try to solve the problem by drawing fast. The catch is, the faster you draw the less accurate you become. Likenesses go, hands look like bunches of bananas, objects and figures begin to merge with one another into an incoherent mess. Nevertheless a line drawn fast seems to contain and express some of the vigour put into its execution, and I am prepared to lose a little coherence in the pursuit of a degree of liveliness. Just as the cartoon ideas must be simplified in the interest of achieving impact, so too must the drawing.

There are many influences on my drawing, but perhaps it is obvious that there have been none as consistent as Vicky's. The quality I admire above all is his ability to sustain this sort of liveliness. His figures seem to jump and rush about on the page.

The scratchy broken lines were apparently swiped across the paper as a boy switches nettles in a country lane. But the carefree execution is deceptive. Mysteriously there is no chaos; each line is doing its job perfectly. Every likeness is unmistakable, every action exactly expressed. For me it is this masterly synthesis of deadly accuracy with dashing vivacity which makes his work outstanding.

Both Low and Vicky were superb simplifiers. The props and settings of their cartoons are masterpieces of economy which the most laid-back Japanese Zen master would be proud of (always assuming Zen masters ever allow themselves to feel proud). Both Low and Vicky make brilliant use of broad areas of black. This may be used to gain two objectives at once. A figure in a black suit or conversely a white figure against a black background stands out stark and clear. At the same time, if it contains bold black areas the cartoon as a whole will hold its own against the busy headlines and vivid photographs of a modern newspaper.

I still have not quite answered the question of how one 'gets' ideas for cartoons. Instead, I am describing how to put oneself in the way of an idea once one becomes aware, in Jonathan Miller's delightful phrase, that there is a joke scurrying around somewhere behind the skirting board of one's mind. The trick is to feed in each day as much information about current events as you can comfortably retain. This information comes from daily newspapers, radio news bulletins and (sometimes) fellow journalists. At the same time as you are accumulating possible subjects, you are winnowing out as many as you can. This theme has been dealt with too recently; that one is still too fluid to risk commentary on; yet another is too little established for many readers easily to comprehend; and so on. Eventually, only one or two ideas remain. What happens then is that the sensible, practical, observable gathering of information ceases, and the imagination must be allowed to slip its moorings and take off. It is the moment that James Thurber said was the most difficult part of his job – that is, persuading his wife that he was working when he was just sitting there gazing out of the window.

Of course, I have learnt a few tricks for those times when visibility is bad and flying conditions are poor. Political cartoonists cannot stockpile ideas because they are tied to current news, but they can stockpile ideas for ideas. I have in my office a great number of picture-books, collections of cartoons, and encyclopaedias. These I can flick through in search of inspiration. I buy postcards of famous pictures that may be useful, and cut pictures from magazines. I pin my own abandoned sketches on the wall in case they can be recycled, and I have cutting books and can reuse old ideas. In my mind I think of this as cobbling together a cartoon. It sometimes feels as if I am hammering a resisting idea into shape. I labour this point a little in order to make another. I think it is sometimes mistakenly believed that cartoonists range, Jove-like, over the political world, thunderbolts in hand, coolly choosing targets. It is not quite like that when you are doing a cartoon every day. In quiet desperation, you are down on the ground scrabbling for ideas and pathetically relieved when one comes along.

From time to time in this description of the work of a political cartoonist, I have used the words *comic, humorous, joke, lighthearted*, and so on. It may have given the impression that we are forever trying to be funny. In fact, in holding up their particular kind of mirror, cartoonists are quite as likely to be reflecting the anger, dismay or grief their fellow citizens are feeling as they are to be indulging a taste for disrespectful frivolity. Cartoonists deal with the themes of death and loss and pain as well as with more cheerful aspects of contemporary life. It is partly for this reason that I do not like the distinction between fine and comic art that we in Britain are inclined to draw. If both may be concerned with the same themes, and both constitute a search after some form of truth, as Caracci made clear, both should be regarded as art. We might then be able to make a more rewarding and proper distinction between good art and bad art.

I ought to confess that, in common with most political cartoonists I know, I studied painting at art school. And if I am asked, as I often am, how do you become a political cartoonist, the answer to this one is quite clear. It is to go to art school and learn to draw.

# Chapter 7

# Buster Keaton and the play of elements

## Robert Goff

> If we know the machine, everything else, that is its movement, seems to be already completely determined.
>
> We talk as if these parts could only move in this way, as if they could not do anything else. How is this – do we forget the possibility of their bending, breaking off, melting, and so on?
>
> Philosophy ... leaves everything as it is.
>
> Ludwig Wittgenstein

In one of his early comedies (*The Frozen North*, 1922) Buster Keaton enters the log house of a woman he desires, gestures his intentions menacingly, and then from the window notices her husband approaching. Buster places himself against the wall and puts an arm into the brackets across the wall and door, making his own limb into a door-bar. This rash move fits into a plot untypical of Keaton which parodies the now-forgotten westerns of William S. Hart, and it also begins a gag which is purely Keaton's. The camera view shifts outside the house to show the husband striding towards the door, and then takes us back inside to see Buster with his door-bar arm in place and body braced in readiness. While his ridiculous gesture furthers the parody, our curiosity is also pressed: what will happen to his arm? Suddenly the door opens inward, and – of course! – Buster's arm bends naturally at the elbow, which now presents itself spontaneously as a door-hinge. He looks amazed, but instead of puzzling about his arm he wonders at the door – looking it over and tentatively swinging it, in utter amazement that a door could so transform an arm.

Set within the visual intensity of silent cinema, this gag relies upon the way we see things on the screen. There, in a black and white two-dimensional world where depth is a subsidiary illusion, things first appear before us on the same plane as lighter or darker elements. When these screen things are then made familiar by a customary analogy to real things, we see each of them in a discrete depth to be this or that. But when the action invokes the screen plane, as it does so often in Keaton's work, things enter a configuration that stresses the manner of their becoming visible. There we are already a bit disposed to take an arm for an unbendable object such as a door-bar, and a door for another flat plane like a movie screen, which may suddenly grant a different form of existence to things appearing on its surface. When the door opens and the arm bends, the gag forms a dual surprise revealing the way each has entered the realm of photographed and projected things.

Another early version of Keaton's characteristic sight humour occurs in *One Week* (1920): as Buster uses his car to pull a two-storey house down the street and across the screen the tow cable breaks. He then backs up the car and nails it to the house. Hammering together a visible mechanical connection stands humorously alongside the even greater arbitrariness of establishing connections and disconnections between profiles on the screen.

The mobility of things in the filmed world extends to the viewer's orientation. The short comedy, *Cops* (1922) has Buster pursued through the city by policemen. Down a street he runs, towards camera and viewer, coming upon a tall ladder leaning against a solid wooden fence that borders the pavement. He climbs the ladder past the top of the fence, and in order to frustrate pursuit begins to tip it over towards the other side. However, a cop catches the lower rung as it rises, prompting

Buster to balance the weight of the cop by crawling out to the ladder's end over a vacant lot. The ladder tips back and forth like a seesaw until another cop appears below Buster's end, prompting a move back to the centre where he then shifts as necessary to balance increasing numbers of cops pulling at one end or the other. From his vantage point he sees a large group of cops coming towards the street side of the fence, so he scoots once more to the ladder-seesaw's other end and hunches down into a projectile shape, ready for launching. When the superior force breaks the balance, he flies through the air, for the moment clear of pursuers.

This scene shows a ladder changing into a bridge, then into a lever, a seesaw and a catapult. At the same time it shows the Keaton figure passing from horizontal fleeing to climbing to weight-balancing to projectile flight, all in fascinating modulation of active and passive. In the arm–door–bar gag the cinematic element was the screen plane; here it also includes camera placement. Change in camera position and angle of view not only informs us about Buster's inventiveness, but gets us up the ladder, hovers us over the fence looking back and forth, and finally throws us out of this scene and into the next. On this level, of the mobilized point of view, we may say that Keaton's work takes advantage of comic possibilities presented by the very nature of cinema. From the film viewer's point of view, cuts and changes of scene occasion leaps (and possible falls), new camera angles mean twists and turns, and change from distance to close-up implies a new development in a chase.

The feature-length *Sherlock, Jr* (1924) recognizes this explicitly when Buster the movie projectionist falls asleep in his booth and dreams his way into the movie being shown: he gets bruisingly tossed between scene cuts. He falls from a porch to a garden bench, then into a busy street, then to the edge of a cliff, then to being surrounded by lions, and so on, in what can be taken as a caution on the hazards of advancing a story's demands without regard to the nature of cinematic presentation. (Keaton knows better than to have Buster simply dreaming the movie with himself in it. Just before these abrupt displacements Buster is thrown bodily out of the screen back into the audience by the movie character whose role he interrupts. He finds it difficult to work his way into the dream movie. For Keaton the creative potential of film cannot be comprehended in easy comparisons with dreaming.)

If on the basis of gags and scenes like these we ask, 'Who is this Buster Keaton figure on the screen?,' the answer cannot be a person or character, as it can, for example, with Charlie Chaplin, whose conspiracy with the audience reinforces his mimetic control. In the early *Dough and Dynamite* (1914), a blob of dough gets treated as boxing gloves, bracelets, quicksand, a mallet, a slingshot, a discus and a chair, completely under Chaplin's magic touch.[1] For such fun the dough needs him, and our enjoyment depends upon him. In contrast, Keaton's arm, door, ladder, camera and screen summon Buster and ourselves each from its own direction. Buster blinks, astonished, and our laughter carries a similar astonishment, but one which is our own and not mediated by a comic personality. While Keaton pays respect to the screen's illusion- and image-making role, Chaplin's virtuosity overtakes the screen (which for him, as has been widely noted, could equally well be a stage).

On another point of Chaplin–Keaton comparison, while their comic profiles both include walking and running, the 'little tramp' has the more specifically characteristic gait, a jerky process of outward toes, picked-up feet and a pronounced swing at the knees, producing a stiff side-to-side motion of the torso. We may wonder whether Chaplin conceived this as a mime of the way those early movies made people look when they walked, but whatever the intent, his screen walk forms an ingenious comment on life at so many frames per second: speeded-up and fragmented, yet strutting in the face of it all. This both embodies and responds to the modern times experienced by movie-goers at first hand; and it also communicates Chaplin's way of regarding film as such, in knowing conspiracy with his audience.

If any aspect of gait characterizes Keaton, it is the transformation of gait, as when in *Go West* (1925), wearing a (presumably red) devil's costume, he begins to lead a herd of cattle through the streets of Los Angeles. The cattle increase their pace, and his deliberate stroll evolves before our eyes into a fleeing headlong dash. Or again, his pace shifts when he sees that the cannon whose fuse he has just confidently lit has swung to point straight up (*The General*, 1926). Anything – physical, animal, human – with an approach seen to be inevitable will likely cause Buster to change pace, not just in response to the object, but in a way that engages the whole scene.

Keaton's walking and running, indeed all his motions, refer to forces beyond himself. When (in *Cops*) Buster sprints around a corner in the distance, chased towards the camera by a dark mass of uniformed policemen, his tiny figure inscribes a round, formal arc in the middle of the intersection instead of a corner-cutting turn more efficient for a real chase. His line of motion holds viewer, streets and police together in shifting play on the screen. Since the Keaton figure should be understood as a personality or character, then *what* is he? His forceful presence in the screen's moving geometry holds a part of the answer, but something must also be said about the kinds of subject and occasion he chooses for his motions.

Keaton's major silent films have recurrent scenes which may be called portraits. Usually concentrated at the beginning, but also occurring throughout, occasionally right up to the end, they present profiles or stance-takings, sometimes of a kind of role he is portraying, sometimes of a whole situation with a number of people, and sometimes of machines in their worlds, machines such as locomotives and ships. The role portrait may be of a bored young man so rich and spoiled that a servant must flick his cigarette ash; or of someone poor, hungry and friendless; or of occupations such as railroad engineer, cowboy or boxer. Buster always dresses perfectly for the pose he strikes.

The situation portraits are arranged with concern for social and historical credibility. We recognize them easily as a nineteenth-century southern US clan feud, a young man trying to propose marriage to his girl in her small-town drawing-room, people sitting on a train or bus, ranch hands at the dinner table, or a boxing match. Some of these portraits are quite ordinary, some dramatic. Keaton's great machine characters, the locomotive *General*, the ocean liner *Navigator*, and the river steamboat *Stonewall Jackson*, receive the form of respect often accorded human actors in silent features, with subtitles announcing them in their first scenes. The locomotives appear in appropriate surroundings with fuel sources, water tanks, track and switches. The ships' portraits include their apparatus, such as gangways, life preservers and anchors, and they always engage a ship's essential medium, the water.

Why should this extensive array of scenes come under the single heading of the portrait? First, because each captures typical figures, events and objects, showing them in what seems their best light. Also, any one of them could be a still picture. The view of the *Atlantic and Western Flyer*, shown in the first shot of *The General* moving along the tracks past the trees, seems as if it could be framed and placed on a wall. A bit later in the same film, the view of citizen volunteers lined up to fight for the Confederacy has a documentary look. Buster with boxing gloves in *Battling Butler* (1926) strikes the pose of a famous illustration of John L. Sullivan, and the baseball sequence of *College* (1927) has him standing the way batters were photographed at the turn of the century.

For Keaton's audience the portraits carried an aura of genuineness – 'This is how it is'; 'That's how it was.' They are also the source and continual reference point for his comedy. He submits each of these carefully posed images to a play of large forces, including wind and water, inertia and gravity, but always extending to light and dark, the horizon, angle of view, and other elements articulated by camera and screen. Keaton begins with the socially typical, renders it in portrait as the visually typical, and sets out upon a comic decomposition where elemental forces overwhelm certain social arrangements, and this includes what happens when the familiar look of things gets caught up in cinematic vision.

In his great essay, 'The work of art in the age of mechanical reproduction', Walter Benjamin talks about how film, by its processes of representation, liberates viewers from the traditional auras attached to things.[2] The aura of something proclaims its origin and value, restricts who can properly use and understand it, and sets conditions for its display and appreciation. For Benjamin, ritual objects show the original form of aura: they are to be handled only during sacred occasions by persons with priestly authority. During the Renaissance, works of art became the chief bearers of aura, accompanied by typical concerns about their uniqueness, authenticity and conditions of display. By extension, natural things and scenes, a river valley for instance, acquire auras conveying special historical and cultural significance. In the current age the aura of something, whether or not it has religious or artistic function, is its accom-

plished and given meaning, prior to our actual present relation
to the thing. On Benjamin's account, film breaks free of aura
because it is reproducible for any audience without regard to
circumstance; indeed the conditions of its display make a virtue
of reproducibility and mass appeal. It also liberates because its
aesthetic structure is montage, whose only tradition is a manner of arranging the juxtaposed images. In montage each image
loses uniqueness by being suddenly opened to the presence of
the other images in the work. The process of film-making forms
montage out of persons and events: for example, an actor before
the camera, instead of portraying an integral role in living
encounter with an audience during a unique performance, receives back from the camera a reflection of his own contingency
and irresolution. Benjamin notes a remark by Pirandello that
an actor before the camera feels the same kind of estrangement
each of us feels before his own image in the mirror.[3] Out there on
the screen, beneath illusions of character, we see an actor-
person as a fragment of montage. Any expected continuity of
aura between who or what is photographed and the images seen
in a complete film has been broken many times over by choice of
camera placement, shooting out of sequence, editing, and the
many other technical processes characteristic of film production. To Benjamin this is no loss, but an appeal to freedom and
imagination:

> By close-ups of the things around us, by focusing on hidden
> details of familiar objects, by exploring commonplace
> milieus under the ingenious guidance of the camera, the
> film, on the one hand, extends our comprehension of the
> necessities which rule our lives; on the other hand, it
> manages to assure us of an immense and unexpected field of
> action. Our taverns and our metropolitan streets, our offices
> and our furnished rooms, our railroad stations and our
> factories appeared to have us locked up hopelessly. Then
> came the film and burst this prison-world asunder by the
> dynamite of the tenth of a second, so that now, in the midst
> of its far-flung ruins and debris, we calmly and
> adventurously go traveling.[4]

Returning to Keaton, loss of aura and the consequent release of kinetic vision are funnier than theoretical discussion makes them sound. In an early short (*The Boat*, 1921), Buster goes to sea with his wife and children on their home-made boat. A storm comes up, so he goes out on deck, picks up a telescope – the long telescoping kind – and takes a look-out's posture. However, the telescope flexes at each joint, drooping drastically in a downward curve from his eye. Then, in a move redeeming his relation to the implement, Buster turns around and stoops over, looking down into the eyepiece of the still-curved telescope whose seeing end now points back between his legs towards the horizon. In a sort of insight through hindsight, Buster achieves comic use of the instrument by shaping his body in response to possibilities of line and view offered in a new-found 'gravity-telescope'. Of course the scene's humour may include its registering the telescope's phallic aspect, but this does not limit the significance of the gag. Chaplin would seize the telescope and adapt it to a mimetic strategy; Keaton always seeks a comedy of things beyond his ability to dominate them. Things change in his presence mostly on their own initiative.

The opening sequence of the feature *College* decomposes a portrait aura by means of climatic elements that lead to other elements. Buster and his proud mother (shown together in portrait) walk through a soaking downpour to his high-school graduation ceremony (another portrait). When they arrive there are few seats left, and he must find a place by himself off to the side up against a radiator. With close-ups the camera establishes that during the ceremony his new suit is in the process of shrinking, so that when the time arrives for his valedictory address he looks like a child who has far outgrown his clothes. With typically serious valedictorian gestures, young Buster embarks on his speech, entitled 'The curse of athletics'. Warming to the subject, he leans admonishingly towards the audience, right and left. The shrunken suit, rigidly binding his legs and torso, lets him lean and sway far to each side with his feet remaining flat. In their chairs behind, the old frock-coated faculty gentlemen incline back and forth in time with Buster, the better to follow his message. Their measured leanings fill the screen with lines more telling than any subtitle.

We have noted that although the portraits from which Keaton begins his comedy are of course part of his motion pictures, he

composes them as if they were still pictures. By contrast, there
are still pictures of Keaton that could just as well be motion
pictures, i.e. still pictures containing at once the whole movement, from conventional portrait to decomposition by elemental
forces to redeemed or resolved vision. In a promotion still for
*The Navigator* (1925) which is not part of the actual film, Buster, wearing sailor attire except for the flattened hat that forms
a portrait of the Keaton clown, assumes a nautical pose both
conventional and extraordinary. He stands upon a ship's rigging, or somehow extends out from the rigging affixed only by
his feet – and this perceptual difficulty, about whether he stands
upon or is affixed to, is important for the picture's effect. We see
more than one portrait here: in fact there are at least four, in a
montage quite magical. First, part of a typical ship with a sailor
look-out in its rigging; second, a clown superimposed (by means
of the hat) upon the sailor; third and fourth, the sailor clown
taking simultaneously the shapes of two different nautical
things, a figurehead for a ship's prow, and a sextant. Without
moving, Buster brings the ship into cinematic play and also
initiates the viewer into the active differences which compose a
ship's perspective.

Another moving-still picture used to promote *The Navigator*
shows Buster inside a deep-sea diving suit with an enormous
heavy helmet. His face appears in a watery blur behind the
glass, with an eloquently minimal look suggesting neither
desperation nor resignation but perhaps something essential to
both. The diving suit loses aura while being opened to its pos-
sibilites as a prison, as an aquarium for a strange marine being,
or even as a coffin-with-a-view. (Interestingly, Keaton nearly
asphyxiated while filming the diving suit scenes. He was doing
a gag that had him smoking with the helmet on, and inside with
the cigarette he could not get the helmet off. He was saved by
someone chancing to notice that his struggles were serious.)

These concentrated images show that Keaton's gaze (not 'expression', which suggests personal character, a category usually
inadequate for the Keaton figure[5]) enters into the large forces
loosed upon portrait poses. Many scenes have Keaton taking a
vantage point – to get out of a predicament, solve a puzzle or
define a view for the camera. He looks intently and inquisitive-
ly, his gaze often establishing a horizon. If he can gaze this way

on behalf of the camera, does his gaze ever turn away from the photographable world and towards the camera itself? There is a remarkable scene in *Steamboat Bill, Jr* (1928), where Buster as Bill, Jr is hauled by his father into the haberdasher's to buy a hat to replace his un-steamboatmanlike beret. He tries on some hats, with the father casting each aside. Then the camera takes the role of mirror, and hats of different styles are handed to Buster by the salesman off-screen. In what is only a matter of a few seconds for each, he deals with succeeding hats by studying himself in the camera mirror, first registering an expression appropriate for a wearer of the particular hat and then reacting to it. (For the audience of the 1920s this portrait comedy was even more subtle because the hats and poses resembled certain film figures of the day.) Throughout, the anxious father looks into the mirror trying to find an image of his son that he can stomach. Buster has been studying the camera in light of the way it is studying him, showing that Keaton does not exempt it from being drawn into a play of comic forces. He takes the camera, along with the audience's typical regard for it (which is, precisely, a disregard) as a received portrait open to a returning, reflective gaze.

Another point where Keaton's gaze meets camera and *mise-en-scène* head on is the concluding scene of *Sherlock Jr*, which has Buster holding his girl in the projection booth and looking out at the movie for guidance on gestures of marriage proposal. He watches the couple on the screen as the hero takes the girl's hand, and so he takes his girl's hand. Step by step he follows the movie couple, putting a ring on his girl's finger, then kissing her. Finally he looks towards the screen for the next move and, in a situation recalling the earlier dream sequence that threw him scene to scene, he sees the couple sitting happily in a domestic setting with twin babies. The last shot of the film leaves Buster holding his girl and confusedly staring out (at screen, camera and us), scratching his head. Between those closing portraits he had just watched, something was cut.

Like his fellow silent film comedians, Keaton had to solve the problem of how to put together comic scenes to form a feature-length film. Chaplin simply left the problem exposed in the form of indefinite connections between episodes, relying upon the brilliance of each episode to diminish any sense of narrative

discontinuity. Even just after seeing a Chaplin silent, who re-
members much about the story or any of its characters except as
they reflect upon the actions of the master mime? Harold Lloyd
held audiences throughout his features by strongly integrating
his comic figure with the story, tapping a preoccupation of the
day concerning a small-town young man's chances for success.
This gained him larger audiences in the 1920s than either
Chaplin or Keaton, and it also explains why his films now look
more dated than theirs.

Keaton's approach to the problem arises from his practice of
beginning films with portrait poses. Even though they may last
only a few moments, we have recognized them, and what follows
in the film acts upon that recognition. Images of a bored or
friendless young man, of a feud between families, an interrupted marriage-proposal, a locomotive or steamboat, not only
get dealt with in a Keaton story, they are also worked upon
visually and kinetically, in the process making our point of view
a part of the action. Three of his features, *Our Hospitality*
(1923), *The General* and *Steamboat Bill Jr*, show especially well
the inclusiveness of his vision.

The story of *Our Hospitality* concerns a blood-feud, with Buster initially unaware that returning to claim his inheritance
makes him the target of gun-wielding males of the Canfield
family. The time is the 1830s, and for an American audience one
of the portraits against which the comedy plays is a conventional picture of national history where the landscape is rough
and passions are simple. The opening scenes show typical cos-
tumes, weapons and modes of conveyance, with the camera
approaching them as sources for gags.

Buster rides a toy-like archaic railway train from New York
to the South, and this journey forms an exploration of the train
world preliminary to *The General*, made three years later. In
the first part of *Our Hospitality* the train itself moves the story,
letting Buster meet the girl of the film (who turns out to be the
daughter of the family who wants him dead), taking him towards unwitting encounter with his would-be killers, and providing the framework for train gags. The bumpy track is shown
causing the rear axle and wheels of the last car to work loose,
something already established as a general possibility, since
the cars of this train are fragile stage-coaches awkwardly

mounted upon heavy flanged wheels. The wheels slide backwards until they are free, disappearing off screen to the right while the coach drops and spills its passengers. On the tracks behind the disabled coach a fist-shaking argument develops between coachman and engineer, when suddenly they are swept off their feet from the right by the errant wheels rolling back across the scene. This business is more subtly funny, with comedy of subject grounded in comedy of sight, because the moment of the returning wheels coming into view is defined by the edge of the screen.

Given Keaton's numerous railway scenes focused upon people and vehicles going down tracks, it is worth suggesting a relation in his work between the physical–mechanical necessities of such subject-matter and the temporal necessities presented to him as a film-maker, in the frame-by-frame succession of exposed film and other track-like realities of production such as short sequences and story-lines. He was both a lifelong tinkerer and gadget-maker who in old age reflected that he might have become an engineer, and a former vaudevillian who had to adapt his stage talent to the different time world of feature-length films. What more practical way to overcome the discontinuity-making tendency of comic scenes to close in upon themselves than building them around actual vehicles of transport, machines like trains, ships, or in the case of *Sherlock Jr*, the motion picture projector? From a conventional serious viewpoint the precision and regularity of these machines seem necessary – we see them capable only of activities consistent with their intended functions. When in Keaton's films machines are placed in surprising relation to weather and horizon or to cinematic connectives such as cutting and screen plane, the usual expectations about necessary function are released into a play of elements, the same play that comically decomposes traditional aura-bound portraits.

While some Keaton features do not concentrate upon machines, they do concern social structures with machine-like necessities. For *Battling Butler*, these are typically fixed conventions of getting and staying married and also training for a championship boxing match. For *Seven Chances* (1925), they are the time- and money-imposed necessity to propose marriage when there is no time for Buster to establish credibility, i.e. to demonstrate his love. In *Go West*, which does include train sequences, they are the demanding routines of a working cattle ranch and then those of a large city. *College* is concerned with the visible conventions and rules of collegiate sports.

Of course the archetypal device for deriving comedy from necessity in film has been the chase, and while Keaton did not invent the film chase, he designed and enacted some memorable ones. As already suggested by the scene (in *Cops*) of a pursued Buster rounding a corner in formal geometric fashion, for him the significance of a chase reaches beyond its human figures, by drawing a line or in other ways establishing visual relationship. Indeed, a large-scale chase forms most of *The General*, whose main figures are more the railway locomotives than the people they carry. However, before we turn to *The General*, a further look at *Our Hospitality* can demonstrate Keaton's probing of distance and connection by means of the chase.

After the train ride the film divides between, on one side, a running series of gags in the house of the charming Canfields, who want to kill Buster but who are also bound by traditional hospitality not to harm a house guest, and, on the other side, a chase which goes through wilderness towards a waterfall. In the second part Buster runs through the forest to a cliffside, down which he climbs until he reaches a ledge where lack of footing leaves him trapped. Overhead an armed Canfield brother discovers where his prey has gone and asks a mining prospector to lend him a rope so he can get a shot at Buster. He throws the rope over the side, and Buster, thinking he is being rescued, ties it around his waist and swings over to a better perch, which then provides Canfield a clear shot. Buster sees him taking aim and recoils out of sight, stumbling so that Canfield, who has tied his end of the rope around his waist, is jerked off the cliff. An interested Buster watches the rope sail down, followed by the person attached to it. After himself being jerked into the fall, he passes Canfield caught on a tree, who is jerked once more into the fall. Finally, in a dizzying view from above, the two plummet, connected by rope, in the water far below.

In the visual economy of *Our Hospitality* the rope takes over the connective work of the earlier railway track. If the film were diagrammed into the lines holding it together, and it does lend itself to such a diagram, the first line would be the track, followed by desperate lines of gaze and glance taken while plotting murder or survival, then by the rope sequence just described, then by lines of river rapids where Buster and the girl are caught drifting one after the other towards doom. The final and spatially resolving line is formed by a clean arc Buster describes swinging on the rope to pluck the girl from disaster at the waterfall's edge.

At the very end of *The General* comes a revealing gag during Buster's reunion with his girl, a gag which gathers together the whole film with its impressively wide-ranging scenes. The story concerns different kinds of love: first, Buster's love for his locomotive, *General*; second, his love for the girl Annabel Lee; and third, their love for their country, the Civil War Confederacy. The last intrudes on the others because Buster's duty to remain an engineer prevents his enlisting as a soldier, so that Annabel considers him unpatriotic. The background for the gag in the couple's eventual reunion begins early in the film on the huge connecting-shaft between the drive wheels of Buster's locomotive. He sits alone on the shaft lost in discouragement at his rejection for military service, which has just been followed by Annabel's command that he not speak to her again until he is in uniform. Then the locomotive slowly starts to move, its connecting-shaft's strokes carrying him gently in wide wheeling arcs off the screen, as if echoing the form of his thoughts. While Buster registers delayed surprise, the locomotive has none the less given a comforting gesture. Most of his actions in the story arise from devotion to this open, trustful being.

The major portion of the film shows the chase which results from Buster's locomotive being stolen and taken across the battle-lines by Union spies, with its scenes placed on or near the railroad tracks, exploring in detailed rhythm everything imaginable about moving trains and people on them. These scenes present a comedy of gravity, inertia, and lines of sight. The concluding gag returns the couple to the locomotive on whose connecting-shaft they now sit together, Buster wearing a new officer's uniform received in recognition of his railroading heroism. They embrace to kiss, but as soldiers walk by, Buster must salute, his arm crossing in front of the embrace. They embrace once more, and are again interrupted by an obligatory salute. A frustrated Buster looks up and sees in the distance a large group of soldiers headed towards them from the encampment down the tracks. Anticipating necessity, he changes places with Annabel, and as the line of soldiers walks by he salutes repeatedly with his outside arm, allowing them at the same time to get on with the kiss. (This gag takes the same direction as the one in *Cops* when Buster sees the larger force of policemen coming and creates a catapult, turning their arrival towards a happier use.) With this image the picture closes on a note of tenderness harmonizing the couple's love with the visual demands of patriotism, a harmony that includes the locomotive reposing steadfastly behind the couple it has helped reunite. Buster's method for continuing the embrace shows he has learned from forces encountered during the locomotive chase. Now he no longer needs to sit on the engine's arm awaiting its reassuring stroke, but can pull himself and the scene together by responding to available elements.

It would be a mistake to use the saluting episode to argue that Buster stoically accepts a world of machine-like necessity. Nor does he 'humanize' machines by adapting them to himself. In Keaton's films machines and implements live in their own worlds, each with characteristic atmosphere and requirements. His careful attention to these screen-filling beings reveals their separate dignity and benign desire for our respect. This is shown at the most breathtaking moment of *The General*, which comes at the end of the chase when we witness the fate of the pursuit locomotive *Texas* starting across the burning Rock River bridge. The bridge gives way and the locomotive with its tender writhes in agony during its heavy plunge into the water. While this has been much discussed as a spectacular movie stunt, it can also claim solemn regard as an epic portrait of the dying locomotive. For the sake of comedy, of course, it is followed immediately by a view of open-mouthed and idiotic incredulity on the faces of the Union generals who sent the Texas on to the bridge. In juxtapositions like this Keaton casts the serious necessity of history, i.e. its customary portrait, into joyous relief.

Smaller-scale figurative gags like the one about saluting also have a crucial role in the ending sequences of *Steamboat Bill, Jr.* The story deals with a college boy and his father who have lived their lives apart and who, now together on the father's steamboat, cannot respect each other. It also centres upon the rivalry between a rundown steamboat, with its rough but genuine captain, Bill, Sr, and a gleaming new steamboat whose owner, J. J. King, is an arrogant nineteenth-century capitalist type. A subordinate aspect of the story concerns young Bill's romance with King's daughter.

Things are at a low point: Bill and the girl have been forbidden by their fathers to continue meeting; for his insubordination, Bill has been given a ticket from River Junction back to Boston; his father has been unjustly jailed, Bill then making a mess of trying to free him; and now a rainstorm intensifies. The great storm-cyclone looms, in which all things, including whole buildings, collapse or fly away.

Ahead of the storm, however, comes a fascinating scene which prepares us, connecting it to the story's misfortunes. The morning of his rejection by his father, Bill walks with his suitcase down the main street of River Junction towards the railroad station. We see his girl walking towards him before he does. When he notices her he stops to speak, and then looks down in confusion about what he should say. While his head is down she walks past with a disdainful glance, disappearing into a building. Expecting her to have stopped in front of him, he looks up to speak, but she has vanished. He shakes his head at the *non-sequitur* and, as if the cosmos had joined her in spurning him, slumps off in defeat towards the station. A moment later she emerges from the building, turns back inside and then emerges again, blinking tears and looking down the street after him. Bill's progress is interrupted as the police car taking his father to jail passes him, snagging his case on its fender. He runs after the car, and the case drops from it, tripping him spectacularly. Here, as in so many Keaton films, sudden unusual movement accompanies a moment of decision: seeing his father being wrongly jailed, Bill tears up his ticket, resolving now to help his father. He stands facing us in the foreground and we can see some distance beyond to where his girl stands, still hesitating and looking wistfully after him. In a view that has them side by side but with her deeply in the background, she starts to come forward. But nearing him she changes her mind once more, turning completely around to walk back the way she came. Just then he turns around to go to the station – only the chase for the suitcase had brought him this far – and sees her a few feet ahead walking in the direction he is now taking. Where did she come from? Once again he registers amazement and trudges away, further convinced the cosmos has turned against him. These intricate encounters are set up by means of camera position and focus, and they hold the key to *Steamboat Bill, Jr*, leading its story into the storm sequence, which centres upon Bill's experiences of extreme disorientation.

Amid all the large-scale wind-driven events, at the very eye of Keaton's storm, comes an episode of smaller illusionary movements on a stage set that is open to the air because the surrounding theatre building has blown away. A small sandbag weight suspended from a pulley falls on Bill's head, a magician's trapdoor opens, a ventriloquist's dummy turns its head towards him. He sees a calm riverbank vista and rushes desperately into it only to bounce off a painted backdrop. The stage magic makes an ultimate claim when the eerie-looking dummy suddenly offers itself, sliding into his hands, which juggle hysterically trying to push it away. He runs from the stage out into the scene of large motions, finally to be borne aloft clinging to a tree which flies, roots and all, over the flooding river.

Above and beyond the magic props on the stage, the storm as a whole displays a cinematic magic – in later years Keaton proudly described the cranes and aircraft engines he used to create its effect. And yet these grand effects aim at more than verisimilitude. When the buildings fly away from their foundations and floors there is a mechanical, cut-out appearance that partakes of the same obviousness as the props Bill meets on the stage set. In addition to placing a stage and props alongside a 'real' storm, the storm sequence intermixes illusions peculiar to each: the stage devices really work in the wind, and the cyclone flings about the things of the world like props. By making Bill's struggle against stage magic the focal point of the storm, Keaton declares his own alliance with both natural and cinematic elements. They must be allowed to declare themselves, and in his work neither film director nor comic figure is permitted to efface them. Instead of trying wilfully to overcome the storm's effects, Bill literally rides them out, letting the soaring tree carry him towards the boat, and letting the floodwaters and the boat's momentum break his father out of the sunken jailhouse. The storm enjoins a receiving and affirming of elements, with storm gags taking things on the fly, and with actions penetrating the frontal illusion of stage and film sets.

The concluding scenes show Bill using long ropes in order to control the boat's engine and save his father. While his appearance of virtuosity may tempt a conclusion that he now becomes a typical hero, dominating a machine that had previously defeated him, what he does can be better understood as an affirming of the rope and its own kind of space, with their offer of connective possibility for vision and story. There is a revealing moment just after the storm: Bill finds himself aboard the *Stonewall Jackson*, which is without its crew, and so he must work alone with the boat. His first job, to be accomplished in haste because rising water threatens to drown his father in his cell, is to tie control levers in the engine room to his position in the wheelhouse two decks above. Bill takes up a rope and quickly loops it around a long lever handle. When he pulls the rope to tighten it, a perfect hitch-knot results. Then with the same motions he loops a rope around a second lever, but this time when he pulls, it falls away in a loose tangle. His next move tells it all: instead of immediately trying again to tie a second knot, he stops and looks at the successful knot with wonder and respect, as if the rope itself created it. Here we see Keaton characteristically stressing a moment of receptivity at the heart of significant action. Bill gazes upon the rope the same way Buster has upon the opening door in *The Frozen North*, upon the impetuous screen in *Sherlock Jr*, upon ladders and bicycles, boats and locomotives whose presence came to astonish him. There on the boat with the rope Bill has learned to pay attention to a joy in the look of things, something (we must conclude) Buster Keaton himself cared very much to teach us.

In summary: Keaton's understanding of film set him apart from the conventional business of doing funny things on the screen. His fascination for how things work extended to the cinema camera and associated devices, which then allowed him to create a comedy of sight around the difference between how things normally look, and how they can look when photographed in motion. When the look of things is submitted to elemental forces like wind, gravity, or the moving geometry of the screen plane, they are neither reduced to nor explained by those forces – comedy is not metaphysics. Indeed, the things, from telescopes to battle-lines and gestures of courtship, remain themselves, although freed by Keaton's visual expansiveness from auras that would control our responses to them. In his films 'things as they are' move from conventionally fixed images to a condition inviting different points of view, new lines of approach. Here the comic figure does not seek our complicity in searching out objects and victims of humour, but summons us to join him in response both wide-eyed and inventive to a world of changing aspects. Now for a time we 'calmly and adventurously go travelling', happily outside the authority of everyday portraiture.

## Notes

1. As described by Gerald Mast, *The Comic Mind*, Bobbs-Merrill, 1973, p. 70.
2. W. Benjamin, *Illuminations*, translated by Harry Zohn, Schocken Books, 1969, pp. 217–51.
3. In the novel *Si Gira*. Benjamin, op. cit., pp. 230–1.
4. Benjamin, op. cit., p. 236. Written in 1935, this passage may convey unwise optimism about the future of the movie-going society, although Benjamin did acknowledge that film was already being subverted by artificial auras developed to serve class and commercial interests, as for example with the build-up of 'star' personalities.
5. There is a fine picture-book, *The Look of Buster Keaton*, by Robert Benayoun, St Martin's Press, 1983.

# Chapter 8

# The importance of being foolish

## Richard Ward

Have you ever noticed that most administrators or directors are failed versions of what they really wanted to be? Well, I am no exception. I am a failed performer. I chose to sit behind a desk and run a circus school so that I did not have to perform. Yet in Belfast, perform is what I did. I was helped through this daunting experience by something I learnt during training. I was taught that an audience receives not only what they see and hear but also what the performer is feeling. For example, if a juggler drops a ball there is a moment of tension. Now if he is feeling cross or nervous, the audience will also feel this. But if he is relaxed and not worried he can pick the ball up and carry on, without the audience feeling bad or sorry for him and in this way they will enjoy the show more.

My subject is clowning. Clowns come under many different names: clown, jester, fool and so on. These words are virtually synonymous; but for me, the most important of them is fool. The word fool is more universal and encompassing than clown, which is why it was chosen as part of this chapter title and why it has been used in the name of my circus school. Fools are an important part not only of our culture but of virtually all other cultures. They also belong in all aspects of entertainment – the theatre, circus, television, films, festivals, and on the street. All these media have their fools. In addition, of course, each of us has our own fool, but most of us let it out only on very rare occasions, once we have become what we call adult.

The fool is by no means a fool. Shakespeare's *Twelfth Night* put it perfectly: 'This fellow is wise enough to play the fool; And to do that well, craves a kind of wit.' This famous passage might stand as the caption for my chapter. To illustrate the wisdom of foolishness, I shall begin by telling about the clown we all know and remember, then discuss how they came into being, and finally touch on the psychology behind it all. My aim, throughout, is to underline the importance of being foolish.

Today, we are witnessing a revival in clowns, clowning and circus generally, What is being revived is not the clowns we remember from our childhood visits to the circus, but a combination of the much older traditional fools and clowns of antiquity and the clowns that have existed under other names through the centuries – from Harlequin, to Chaplin, to John Cleese. This revival is happening against the backdrop of a century-long growth of huge three-ring circuses, in which the great majority of clowns were reduced from an important role in society to the rank of mere children's entertainers. There were, of course, memorable exceptions: Emmet Kelly, the American tramp clown; Grock, the Swiss king of clowns; Coco, the Russian who worked for many years with Bertram Mills Circus; and the Corali Brothers, who worked as a pair – one clown, and one Auguste.

This brings me to the question: when is a clown not a clown? The answer is, when he is an Auguste. An Auguste is the figure most of us see in our mind's eye when we think of a circus clown – a colourful character with baggy trousers, painted face and a red nose. Augustes have only existed for just over a hundred years. The real clown is the white faced clown, a beautifully dressed, elegant figure who usually possesses a number of skills, (for example, he is often musical). The white faced clown is a direct descendant of Harlequin from the Italian *commedia dell'arte* period.

Now I would like to tell a story about how the Auguste came into being and got his name. About a hundred years ago, a young American acrobat called Tom Belling was messing about in the changing rooms of a circus in Berlin. The story goes that he was entertaining his colleagues by dressing up in ridiculous clothes and wigs, until someone in the group wagered that he would not go down to the ringside looking like that. Well, this was like a red rag to a bull, and off Belling went. Thinking he could get away with wandering around the edge of the ring, things went wrong and he suddenly found himself face to face with the ringmaster. Instead of dismissing him, the ringmaster roared with laughter and gave him a hearty bash on the back. This caught Belling off balance and sent him flying into the ring. Thinking this was part of the show, the audience roared with laughter and shouted 'Auguste! Auguste!', which in German means silly or stupid. And so the clown that most of us know was born, and christened, in Berlin.

This is an amusing story, but it is very difficult to know whether it is true. Either way, however, over the last century clowns have usually worked in pairs or troupes with one white-faced clown and one or more Augustes. The Augustes that worked on their own were called carpet clowns, although this term has more recently been used to describe fill-in clowns who come on between acts to keep the audience amused while the ring hands move things around ready for the next act. There is a third type of clown, of which Emmet Kelly is probably the best-known example, and that is the tramp clown or hobo who, not surprisingly, dresses like a tramp but also has a painted face and red nose. Generally, tramp clowns have been more figures of pathos than most other clowns.

The film-maker Federico Fellini has said:

When I say clown, I think of the Auguste. The two types of clown are in fact the White Clown and the Auguste. The White Clown stands for elegance, grace, harmony, intelligence and lucidity which are posited in a moral way as ideal, unique, indisputable divinities. Then comes the negative aspect, because in this way, the White Clown becomes Mother and Father, Schoolmaster, Artist, the Beautiful, in other words *WHAT SHOULD BE DONE*. Then the Auguste, who would feel drawn to all these perfect attributes if only they were not so priggishly displayed, turns on them ... This is the struggle between the proud cult of reason ... and the freedon of instinct. The White Clown and the Auguste are teacher and child, mother and small

son, even the angel with the flaming sword and the sinner.
In other words they are two psychological aspects of man;
one which aims upwards, the other which aims downwards;
two divided, separated instincts.[1]

This quotation is not just about the difference between the
white-faced clown and the Auguste, but also demonstrates
the difference in status of the two characters. The white-faced
clown exaggerates the qualities of the high-status characters
in society, and the Auguste is demonstrating the 'instinctual
nature' of the lower ranks. Think of Morecambe and Wise, who
are prime examples of this dual relationship. A good servant
would not ever touch his master, yet Morecambe could destroy
his partner's status by slapping his cheeks and then inviting the
audience to laugh.

To me, the outstanding difference between clowning and any
other form of entertainment is that clowns allow us to laugh at
*them*, whereas most forms of comedy make us laugh at other
people – the mother-in-law, the vicar, or whoever. Barbara
Swain once wrote: 'The freedom to indulge in parody and unexpected truth telling, and the additional freedom to be wantonly
licentious without incurring blame are the two privileges of the
fool which make it worth the while of normal men occasionally
to assume his role.'[2] The importance of clowning is that it is an
extremely comfortable form of humour. We the audience do not
have to make judgements as to 'whether we should or should not
laugh'. A good clown very clearly gives us permission to laugh,
usually by looking directly at us, or by making some other
gesture indicating that laughter is in order. Another technique
widely used by clowns to relax an audience is 'audience participation'. This is not unique to clowning, but it is highly characteristic of it. I suppose that a modern equivalent of it would be
television quiz programmes. Audience participation is really an
invitation to the audience to 'come and play'.

Interestingly, when we laugh at clowns we are usually
laughing at them doing normal day-to-day things in an ex-
aggerated or very strange way. I remember one of my teachers
telling me the difference between an ordinary person and a
clown: 'A pianist sits down to play a grand piano and finds that
the seat is too far away from the piano. You or I would pull the

seat up to the piano. But a clown gets up, walks round and pushes the piano towards the seat and then walks back and sits down again.' It is the same with the clown's clothes. These are mostly just exaggerations in either size, shape, fit or (in the case of the white clown) beauty. What I think all this tells us is that, by allowing us to laugh at him, the clown is actually helping *us* to laugh at *ourselves*. Emmet Kelly, the tramp clown, once wrote: 'By laughing at me, the audience really laugh at themselves, and realising that they have done this gives them a sort of spiritual second wind for going back into the battle of life.'[3]

Now for a little of the history of these wonderful characters. As far as we know, clowns have existed as long as people have existed. Hiler Harzberg and Arthur Moss have observed, 'It is reasonable to assume that the first clowning was accidental and that the first clowns were sublimely unconscious as to how funny they were.'[4]

A relatively familiar early example of the clown as an established figure is that of the King's or Queen's jester, or fool. Court jesters were employed ostensibly to entertain, but in fact they usually had a far more important role and a considerable amount of influence. Shakespeare was well aware of this, and perhaps the best example of the most wise fool is to be found in *King Lear*. Without the fool this tragedy of foolish misjudgement would be incomprehensible. The fool's observations on the King's authority point out the absurdity of the King's actions to the audience. This is drama, but there are endless true stories of wise fools and jesters going back through the centuries and right across the world.

One of the earliest stories I could find is from China in about 1000 BC. The story comes from a book called *Clowns* by Douglas Newton:

A Chinese Emperor ... would allow nothing but ten-cash pieces to be minted. No one dared explain the disadvantages of this to him until two of his clowns thought of a comic turn to perform 'for his amusement'. One took the part of a soft-drinks seller, the other the part of his customer. The customer asked for a one-cash drink, and handed over the smallest coin he had – a ten-cash piece. The vendor could not give him any change, for he had no smaller coins either, so,

with a great deal of puffing and blowing, the customer
drank ten big drinks. Then he sighed, and burst out with,
'There! But if the Government made us use those big
hundred-cash pieces I'd have popped!'

The Emperor laughed long and loud – but the next day he
ordered one-cash pieces to be put back into circulation.[5]

From cultured civilizations we can go to the uncivilized and still
find references to clowns. One story of clowns comes from the
native people of Vancouver Island, whose stories have been
preserved for generations through an oral tradition among the
women. Their clowns did not resemble ours in dress (they wore
whatever they felt like), but they were an important part of the
society, as important in fact as the Chief, the dancers or the
poets. In her book *Daughters of Copper Woman*, Anne Cameron
relates the following story:

The people were goin' down to Victoria a lot and tradin' with
Hudson Bay for things they couldn't get anywhere else.
They'd kill seal and otter, more than ever before so they'd be
able to trade the skins, and even though everyone knew it
couldn't last, even though everyone knew the animals
wouldn't be able to survive, nobody seemed willin' to be the
first to not do it. It was like they figured it was gonna
happen anyway, they might as well get some of it for
themselves. And not all of the stuff they traded for was
worth anythin'. You make a long trip with a big bundle of
furs, and you don't feel like bringin' it all home just because
the Hudson Bay man doesn't want to trade for somethin' you
want. More and more the company was just handin' out
junk, and private traders were steppin' in with a few blue
beads and lot of rum, and it was all a real mess.

And this same clown woman, she took herself down to
Victoria and she set up shop right next to Hudson Bay.
Hudson Bay would give beads, so she had bits of busted
shell. They'd give molasses, so she had wild honey. They'd
give rum, so she had some old swamp water. And she just sat
there. That's all she did, was just sit there. And the people
goin' to Hudson Bay saw her, and saw the stuff she had to
trade, and they knew what she was tellin' them. Some of 'em

went inside and traded anyway, but some of them just turned around and went back home, and some of them even went over and traded with her, and she treated them all real serious, took their furs and gave 'em bits of shell and stuff, and they wore it same as they'd 'a wore the beads.

After a while the Hudson Bay man came out to see why hardly anybody had come to trade and he saw her sittin' there and he just about blew up, took himself off to the Governor and complained about the clown woman. The Governor, he took himself outside and had a look and then told the Hudson Bay man a thing or two, and from then on we got good tradin' stuff.[6]

The most important influence on clowns and fools as we know them today was the sixteenth-century *commedia dell'arte*, which originated in Italy and eventually spread across Europe to reach England at the end of the seventeenth century. In her book *Bring on the Clowns*, Beryl Hugill wrote:

> The *Commedia dell'Arte* was, in fact, the comic theatre in which clowns as we know them first appeared.
> Improvisation was its most important characteristic. The actors had their instructions pinned up in the wings of the makeshift theatres in which they performed and were given a brief scenario within which they extemporized. Each of them played a stock character, who was a caricature of some Italian type found in a certain town or region. The most enduring of these characters are Harlequin, Columbine, Pantaloon, Scaramouche and Pierrot.[7]

Another important and remarkable character from this comic theatre was Pulcinella, who on reaching England became Punch, of Punch and Judy fame.

I want to say a little about some of these enduring characters. Pierrot is especially well known. At present the shops are full of pictures of him – in fact my twelve-year-old daughter's room is covered with pictures on the duvet, the lampshade and the wall; but he is most famous as the clown that played at the end of piers at seaside resorts. Harlequin, with his diamond-checked costume, is the direct forerunner of our traditional white-faced clown. Pantaloon was one of the strongest characters from the *commedia*, but we do not see him these days in conventional clowning. Pantaloon was a capitalist; he was greedy, a hoarder, hypochondriac and a lecher. Shakespeare's Shylock was a Pantaloon character; and so, I suppose, in modern times is John Cleese in 'Fawlty Towers'.

When *commedia* came to England it gradually turned to pantomime, with the Harlequin character as the most important element. Over a period of time the Harlequinade was gradually dropped from pantomime to leave it as we know it today; and gradually the Harlequin character developed into the circus clown. Probably the most important character in this transition was Grimaldi, another famous clown whose heyday was at the beginning of the nineteenth century. It is from Grimaldi that the nickname 'Joey', still used today, came to be a synonym for clowns. According to Charles Dibdin, 'The present mode of dressing up clowns and painting their faces, was then invented by Mr Grimaldi, who, in every respect, founded a New School for Clowns.'[8]

We have looked at one thread from *commedia* to pantomime to Grimaldi and the white-faced clown. Another thread from *commedia* connected pantomime, vaudeville and the silent movies. Buster Keaton, the Marx Brothers and Charlie Chaplin were all great clowns, and they drew heavily on the clowning comedy that had been developed over centuries and refined in pantomime and vaudeville.

Before I leave Harlequin and the *commedia* period, there is one other heritage that I should mention, and that is slapstick. Not only did the form come down to us through *commedia*, but also the name. Harlequin always carried with him a sword, with which he liberally hit other people in the cast. To make this seem effective without the risk of hurting people, his sword was made from two thin pieces of wood with a small gap between, which gave a resounding crack when it struck home. This later became known as a *slapstick*, and the term eventually outlived the instrument.

We have now talked about clowns and clowning from a number of aspects, but why is all this so important? What impact can clowns have on our society today, and what about the clown that each of us has inside ourself?

Even in our society, by virtue of their history clowns have a freedom that we may envy. They can do what they want, and we cannot. They have the capacity to stay with a problem; in fact, this is often one of the funniest things about them. Too often, both personally and nationally, we put off finalizing things to avoid having to take the next step. Frequently, it is easier to stay with the present problem, than to have to think where we might go if or when it is solved. Television soap operas help to reinforce this by keeping us comfortable in our problems. The general formula for soap operas appears to be to go from a neutral state to something a little friendly; then back to neutral; then on to something a little hostile; and so on. The plot is always on the move, but never too disturbing; viewers move from problem to problem and never actually solve anything. The clown, by contrast, is often disturbing precisely because he stays with a problem. He is always extreme, and never escapes into the neutral state. At the same time, he is never worried by a problem; he is not into mental breakdowns, or anything like that. The clown just gets on with solving whatever the problem happens to be, usually in the most ridiculous way imaginable.

A lot of people in our society play clown roles without realizing it. For instance five Canadians recently did a clown routine to demonstrate something to the Government. Because of a temporary petrol shortage the Canadian Government introduced a 50 mph speed limit to save fuel, but after the shortage was over, the limit was never repealed. So, on a five-lane highway five Canadians drove their cars side by side at 50 mph for hours and caused total chaos, not only on that road but on many others. This was a form of clowning: a persistent attempt to solve a problem in an absurd way. This attempt to change the law did not succeed, but at least it made the point.

Many clowns have skills such as juggling, rope walking or acrobatics. What is funny, we may ask, about such skills as these? Even more, what is funny about seeing skills executed badly (think, for example, of that marvellous clown, the late Tommy Cooper). Well the trouble is that today everything is measured by the product. What the audience is appreciating when they watch a skill is the hours and hours of almost obsessive practice that are required before a skill can be executed well. For the most part, however, the audience is unaware of this background; it forgets the extraordinary effort that goes into learning a skill. What the clown does is to remind us of this effort. In his absurdity, he teaches us the true value of skills. How many of us, I wonder, play this part of the clown's role by having an obsession to learn something? Some of the most common examples are probably various kinds of so-called sports or hobbies. These activities have an excellent purpose which the clown is showing us. They raise our spirits, and – if we allow them to – inspire us to new forms of consciousness.

Part of the clown's freedom that we envy is to be ridiculous. In our society today there are a number of people who are prepared to expend a great deal of energy in avoiding work. I do not entirely understand this phenomenon, but it seems that some people will go to any lengths to avoid working even if this requires more effort than actually doing the work. Something rather similar to this that we all do from time to time is to go to great lengths to avoid looking silly, and in a lot of cases ending up looking even sillier than if we had not started. I have recently been on holiday and had the opportunity to watch one of the prime examples of this sort of conduct: changing on a beach. If we just undressed and put our swimming costume on, our private parts would be exposed for perhaps a few seconds, when somebody might just happen to get a glimpse of them. Most probably nobody would even notice; and anyway, who has not seen it all before? But what do we do? In our anxiety to avoid exposing ourselves, we wrap ourselves in towels or other specially designed clothing, within which we attempt to change our clothes. What follows is a form of pure comedy. Usually, after a great deal of struggling, the towel or whatever falls off at the crucial moment; at this moment of exposure, the whole performance becomes a clown routine. I am reminded of a quote from the Bible, 1 Corinthians 3:18: 'Make no mistake about it; if any one of you thinks of himself as wise, in the ordinary sense of the word, then he must learn to be a fool before he really can be wise.'

I should like to end with a quotation; it is Bario's speech from *The Clowns*, by Federico Fellini:

... the state ought to consider opening a school for clowns. No age limit: when a man's got the vocation for it, he can

dedicate himself to it even at forty, and become a clown.
Take an engineer, say. Now if he has the vocation for it, he
can become a clown. University graduates, doctors, lawyers.
They've all been excellent ... It's good for your health to be a
clown, you know. It's good because you can do anything you
like; break everything, tear everthing, set fire to things, roll
on the floor, and nobody ticks you off, nobody stops you. The
children wish they could do what they liked: tear things, set
fire to things, roll on the floor ... and so they love you. We
ought to support them, and encourage them to go ahead
with a good school for clowns, open to children – particularly
to children. That way they could do what they liked, enjoy
themselves and give enjoyment to others. It's a good job, and
if you can do it you earn just as much as you would in an
office. Why do parents want their children to work in offices
and not be clowns? It's all wrong.[9]

Well, the state did not open a school for clowns, so eighteen
months ago in Bristol – *I did!*

## Notes

1. Federico Fellini, *Fellini on Fellini*, translated by Isabel
   Quigley. New York: Delacoste Press/Seymour Lawrence,
   1976.
2. Barbara Swain, *Fools and Folly during the Middle Ages and
   the Renaissance*. New York: Columbia University Press,
   1932.
3. Emmet Kelly, *Clown*, with F. Beverly Kelley. New York:
   Prentice-Hall, 1954.
4. Hiler Harzberg and Arthur Moss, *Slapstick and Dumbbell: A
   Casual Survey of Clowns and Clowning*. New York: J. Law-
   ren, 1924.
5. Douglas Newton, *Clowns*. London: George G. Harrap & Co.,
   1958.
6. Anne Cameron, *Daughters of Copper Woman*, London:
   Women's Press, 1984.
7. Beryl Hugill, *Bring on the Clowns*. New Jersey: Chartwell
   Books, 1980.

8. Quoted in John H. Towsen, *Clowns*. New York: Hawthorn Books, 1976.
9. Fellini, *op. cit.*

# Chapter 9

# Humour as a vehicle for unconventional ideas

## Alexander Kohn

In his well-known Mudfog Papers, Charles Dickens refers to the Mudfog Association for the Advancement of Everything.[1] At one point, Dickens's talented correspondent says,

> I cannot close my account of these gigantic researches and sublime and noble triumphs without repeating a *bon mot* of Professor Woodensconce's.... I was standing by when that learned gentleman, accompanied by the whole body of wonderful men, entered the hall yesterday, where a sumptuous dinner was prepared, and where the richest wines sparkled on the board and fat bucks, propitiatory sacrifices to learning, sent forth their savoury odours. 'Ah – ', said Professor Woodensconce, rubbing his hands, 'this is what we meet for; this is what inspires us; this is what keeps us together and beckons us onward: this is the spread of science, and a glorious spread it is.'

Scientific activity is like play. It may be defined as an output of physical activity without an immediately useful purpose. Its justification, for those who engage in it, is the actual pleasure they derive from it. Why, then, did the British Association for

the Advancement of Science assemble in Belfast for its Annual
Meeting? The novelist David Lodge has the answer:

> The modern conference resembles the pilgrimage of
> medieval times in that it allows the participants to indulge
> themselves in all the pleasures and diversions of travel
> while appearing to be austerely bent on self-improvement.
> To be sure, there are certain penitential exercises to be
> performed – the presentation of a paper, perhaps, and
> certainly listening to the papers of others. But with this
> excuse you journey to new and interesting places, meet new
> and interesting people, eat drink and make merry in their
> company every evening; and yet, at the end of it all, return
> with an enhanced reputation for seriousness of mind.
> Today's conferees have an additional advantage over the
> pilgrims of old in that their expenses are usually paid, or at
> least subsidized.[2]

After this preamble I should like to speak about the sources of
unconventional or perhaps extravagant ideas in science, but
first a few words about my methods. The technique I shall be
using is the so-called 'squid system', which is based on throwing
a lot of confusing dye at the audience to facilitate escape. As an
example of this technique, I quote from a European Public
Health Committee report of the early 1970s: 'The merit of this
report is the future oriented confrontation with the backgrounds against which concrete problems should be projected,
and weighing of these backgrounds against each other.' The
squid system makes use of copious illustrative diagrams. Figure
1, for example, may be used to illustrate any function and result
obtained in the majority of research projects. The projection of
such a diagram on the screen is preceded by the words: 'This
slide simply shows ...'. A more useful slide is shown in Fig. 2.
This is introduced by: 'As you may see ...', following which the
speaker is free to present any existent or non-existent data on
any subject.

My chief qualification as a writer on the subject of humour as
a vehicle for unconventional ideas is that I am founder and chief
editor of the *Journal of Irreproducible Results*, the official organ
of the Society for Basic Irreproducible Research. This journal is

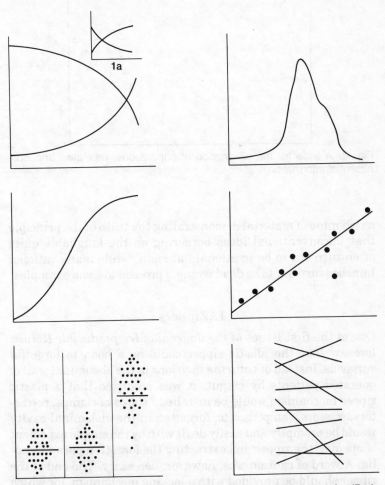

**Fig. 1.** Standardized data display module for information transfer (R. A. Greenwald, *JIR*, **23** (3) (1977) 9).

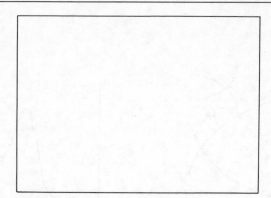

Fig. 2. A slide for the elimination of superfluous, unrelated and non-essential information.

a rich mine of material demonstrating the truth of the principle that unconventional ideas bordering on the laughable quite often turn out to be irrational but right, while many rational hunches turn out to be dead wrong. I proceed to some examples.

## 1. Zippers

One of the first issues of the *Journal of Irreproducible Results* foresaw that the plastic zipper could be a boon to forgetful surgeons. Instead of suturing incisions in the abdominal wall of operated patients by catgut, it was predicted that a plastic zipper mechanism would be installed.[3] Cases of clamps, retractors, scissors, tampons, etc. forgotten in the abdominal cavity would be promptly and easily dealt with by the simple expedient of opening the zipper and extracting the forgotten paraphernalia. A word of caution was, however, necessary. The end of the zipper should be provided with a locking mechanism, for which only authorized personnel would have the key. This precaution is very important, inasmuch as the use of Freudian techniques for testing one's own interior machinery has already been practised with disgusting results.

Azo Koh's irreproducible zipper predictions thirty years ago became a reality in 1986. B. J. Rubin of YKK Macon, writing in the *New England Journal of Medicine*, urges physicians not to use zippers for medical purposes because they are not sterile and may have on them all sorts of oils, detergents and other chemicals. He ends by saying that as a manufacturer of zippers he cannot be responsible for any injury caused by the use of zippers for medical purposes. However, this letter is followed by a statement from Dr Harlan Stone of the University of Maryland that the use of zippers 'has greatly facilitated reexploration of the abdomen when it is required on an almost daily basis'. He adds that he uses Talon zippers, which are 'less likely to disengage and lead to evisceration in comparison to YKK zippers'.[4]

## 2. Iceberg solution to water problem

Some very important discoveries have been suggested on the pages of the *Journal of Irreproducible Results*. Some of them turned to reality. One interesting idea, described in 1966 by Novick, concerned the solution to the water problem in arid countries, such as Israel.[5] The suggestion was to locate an iceberg of about $10 \times 2 \times 0.2$ km and transport it with the help of several frigates and destroyers, or to construct a special vessel for this purpose. It was calculated that such transport might take a few months and that there would be a loss of about half of the mass of the towed iceberg. Nevertheless, some 1000 million cubic metres of ice would serve to supply the annual water consumption of a country like Israel. In addition, the transport of an iceberg through the Mediterranean was expected to cool the climate. This extravagant idea has led in recent years to an international engineering project financed by some affluent Arab countries, and all the necessary preparations and engineering plans for the transport of icebergs from the Antarctica to Australia or Saudi Arabia have been worked out.

## 3. Refrigerated underwear

An interesting technological fantasy resulting from a paper published in *Nature* twenty years ago and reprinted in the *Journal of Irreproducible Results* became a reality a decade after its publication. The paper, by Ehrenberg and von Ehrenstein of the University of Stockholm, was entitled 'Gonad temperature and spontaneous mutation rate in man'.[6] The study noted that in the fruit fly increase of temperature increases the mutation rate by a factor of 2 for every 6–7°C. The authors wondered if in man, too, the temperature of the gonads might affect the human mutation rate. They therefore conducted a study in a nudist camp, where they had nude and clothed subjects with thermocouples attached to their scrotums. They found that the temperature of the scrotum of nude subjects was about 3°C lower than that of clothed subjects, and calculated that, based on the data from fruit flies, this might result in an increase by 85 per cent of the mutation rate transmitted by the clothed men. The authors concluded: 'If the eugenists regard this increase as dangerous, the design of male clothing will have to be reformed, for example in the direction of the Scottish kilt, or of trousers fitted with a codpiece as used in medieval Europe.'

A correspondent reacted to this paper in the pages of the *Journal of Irreproducible Results* by suggesting the use of cooled underwear made of material suitable for housing a refrigerating circulation system (made of plastic tubes with a refrigerant of high storage capacity such as water).[7] The water would be cooled by a suitable compression system run either on solid state batteries or solar batteries, depending on the climate. We now know that this predicted invention has actually been devised for astronauts.

## 4. How to reduce evaporation

In 1952 Australians made the first attempts to reduce evaporation from lakes and reservoirs by using thin films of inorganic compounds.[8] At that time practical applications did not result from this idea; but a few years later, Dr Stanhill of the Volcani Institute in Israel suggested the use of paper to prevent evaporation.[9] Based on an exponential increase from 1954 onwards of the number of papers on evaporation reduction, the number of journals publishing these papers, the number of reprints, and the size of the pages, Stanhill calculated that the area of the paper used in 1970 was about 70,000 sq. metres. Taking into consideration the reflection coefficient of the paper (0.33, instead of 0.08 for open water) and the areas involved, he calculated that the reduction of evaporation from a surface covered with this amount of paper would save about 52,000 cubic metres of water. He added to this calculation the consideration that the paper for the journals came actually from pine forests: the research published on this topic required about 750 sq. metres of forest per year. Deforestation in arid areas increases the water yield from catchment areas, and about 100 cubic metres of water are saved by reduction of evapotranspiration.

These water savings are completely independent of the contents of the publications. Unpublished papers, i.e. blank paper, would be even better for covering the water and preventing its evaporation. Stanhill's method was criticized in 1975 by Howmiller.[10] He claimed that randomly selected paper from the hydrological literature had a high content of bovine excrement (BX), of the order of about 50 per cent. The paper cover would add to the water at least 44.5 g of BX per sq. metre. This addition of organic matter would lead to eutrophication of bodies of water thus covered with BX-containing paper, though in judicious amounts it might improve the micronutrient contents of shallow ponds.

Quite recent information indicates that the idea of preventing evaporation by covering large bodies of water is being taken very seriously. The most recent serious idea is to cover the surface with polyurethane chips.

## 5. Cancer caused by water and food

Studies on rats by J. M. Williams published in the *Journal of Irreproducible Results* showed that distilled water injected into female albino rats caused breast carcinomas in 4 out of 10 rats within 200 days, while similar injections of saline did not. As to extrapolation to humans, there was not enough evidence that women consume enough water. We may expect, however, that the Food and Drug Administration will establish guidelines as to the maximum safe rate of water consumption per capita for women.[11] Similar rat experiments with about 1000 rats divided into groups of 100 and fed various diets, with Checkerboard rat chow serving as a control, indicated that almost anything else the rats consumed was carcinogenic, including corn on the cob, T-bone steak, baked potatoes, pizza and grilled cheese sandwiches. It is therefore suggested that rat chow be adopted for human consumption. In order to overcome possible objections, this food can be disguised with the help of monosodium glutamate, cyclamate and suitable edible dyes to conform with the current taste of the community.

Is this idea too fanciful? Federal agencies of the USA charged with the responsibility of determining what is good for us have readily accepted studies on rats as being capable of extrapolation to infinity. By this method, the Drug Administration has forbidden the use of cranberries, food dyes, cyclamate, oestrogen and saccharin, though of course tobacco may be freely used by anybody who ignores the government warning on cigarette packages.

## 6. Chicken soup cures all

Let us now take up the subject of chicken soup. Jewish mothers invariably prescribe chicken soup as a remedy for practically any illness. Maimonides postulated that soup made of old chickens was of benefit against chronic fevers, coughs and asthma. The chicken in question (not too small, not too lean and not too obese) should be boiled or stewed with fresh coriander and green fennel, and lemon juice should be added. In 1975, Dr Caroline of the Presbyterian Hospital in Pittsburgh and Dr Schwartz from Cleveland described a case of pneumonia in a forty-seven-year-old patient who dramatically improved upon ingestion of half a quart of chicken soup.[12] When the patient stopped consuming the chicken soup he became gravely ill, and only massive doses of penicillin saved his life. Once again, science is slowly catching up. Saletkhoo and his colleagues have studied the effects of drinking hot water, cold water and chicken soup on nasal mucus velocity and nasal airflow resistance. They found that only chicken soup mobilized nasal mucus, and therefore that it might indeed be beneficial in curing upper respiratory diseases.[13]

These papers started an avalanche of letters to the editors: Yablin and Jacobson announced that they were preparing a paper on 'The preparation and therapeutic efficacy of chicken soup based on a large series of nine grandchildren'. Peckman, from the Chicken Soup Institute in Philadelphia, proposed the hypothesis that soup made of happy (rather than unhappy) chickens would be more beneficial. Professor Green from the

Mayo Clinic reported a successful application of a chicken-derived ointment, named Schmalz, for treatment of impotence. He also stated that he had received a grant from the National Science Foundation for prospective randomized double blind study of this subject, but that he could not find suitable volunteers since everybody wanted to be in the subject rather than the control group. The most amazing proposition, however, came from the head of a department of Sikorsky Aircraft in Connecticut, who suggested that chicken soup research might lead to 'important transfers of technology between the medical and the engineering disciplines' and become a base of a novel aircraft fuel for the Israeli Air Force.

I hope I have given enough examples to prove to you that the *Journal of Irreproducible Results* papers that seem laughable are merely ahead of their times. The *Journal of Irreproducible Results*, of course, is not the only periodical which publishes extravagant ideas that later become true. In a recent issue of the journal *Speculations in Science and Technology*, Sherwood Idso[14] of Arizona shows that his speculative prediction that initial injection of dust into the Martian atmosphere by dust devils would play a crucial role in Martian duststorms has indeed now been confirmed by Viking orbiter observations, as published in *Science*.[15]

## 7. Awaiting creative applications

We have seen that some extravagant ideas have already been realized. Some others, however, are still in the realm of fantasy.

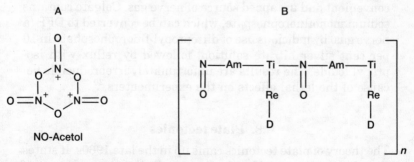

Fig. 3. NO–acetol (a); and its derivative (b)

Let us describe some of these unusual, extravagant ideas which
await creative application.

Two types of new contraceptives have been devised, both
based on the unorthodox use of nitroso compounds, –NO–.[16] One
of these, the NO–acetol (Fig. 3a), has an NO in every position
and has even been improved by opening the ring and substitut-
ing rare metals in it (Fig. 3b), to yield:

$$NO\text{—}Am\text{—}Ti$$
$$|$$
$$Re$$
$$|$$
$$D$$

This new compound when polymerized, that is when repeated
again and again, becomes a very effective contraceptive.

Another as yet unrealized invention is the use of the house
cricket as a temperature sensor in delicate instruments.[17] The
*Journal of Irreproducible Results* was the first to explain the
launching failures of some ballistic missiles by an 'umbilical
complex', that is the detachment of the 'umbilical' cords and
tubes which supply the missile with vital materials before launching leads to launching failure.[18] Again, a very interesting
concept developed by the *Journal of Irreproducible Results* contributors is the *dark bulb*. In contrast to the light bulb, which
*emits* light, the dark bulb *absorbs* radiant energy and therefore
creates complete darkness around it.[19]

Mike Conrad of Berkeley proposes Colgate toothpaste as a
convenient and untapped source of nerve gas. Colgate contains
sodium monofluorophospate, which can be converted to DFP (a
nerve gas) by judicious use of diisopropyl-fluorophosphate in 10
per cent silver nitrate solution, followed by reflux with iso-
propyl iodide. The results are unfortunately irreproducible because of the lethal effects on the experimenters.[20]

## 8. Plate tectonics

The theory of plate tectonics came up in the late 1960s. It states
that the continents drift, relative to each other, because some of

the sea floor on which they are resting disappears into the earth's interior. When one looks at the shape of the continents (Fig. 4), one observes that the continents are tear-drop shaped, a fact which may indicate the direction from which the continents

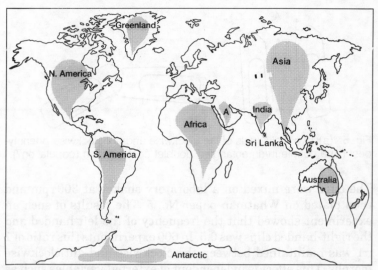

Fig. 4. Continental drip.

came, i.e. so-called continental drip.[21] The continents seem to be flowing north. Since everybody knows that drip is always downwards and not upwards, we must conclude that in the geological past the South Pole was north, and vice versa. The only exception to the drip theory is the anti-drip of Sri Lanka, and perhaps that of Antarctica, but this might be because Antarctica being situated where it is has not made up its mind in which direction to flow. On the base of this new continental drip theory we may expect that in the year AD 1,786,379 all the continents will reunite at the North Pole. It is, however, expected that the gravitational instability caused by aggregation of all continents at the North Pole will cause the earth to 'flip' again, so that the North Pole will once again become the South Pole.

### 9. Morphism of the common paper clip

Schmidtke and Krawczak of Göttingen performed a number of experiments to investigate the quantitative relationship of the two more frequent forms of the common paper clip (Fig. 5a).[22]

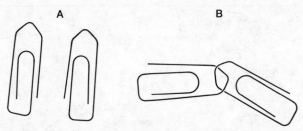

**Fig. 5.** (a) Two individuals of the clockwise and anticlockwise phenotypes; (b) a couple in an entangled doublet configuration (copulation?).

The clips were mixed on a laboratory shaker at 300 rpm and then plated on Whatman paper No. 5. The results of such an experiment showed that the frequency of the left-handed and the right-handed clips was 0.5. In 600 experiments this ratio of 1 : 1 was maintained between the clockwise and anticlockwise morphs. This effect is independent of external variables such as temperature and incubation periods as well as of strain origin. Since this process of segregation is practically instantaneous, it contradicts Einstein's Special Theory of Relativity. Occasionally, tangled doublets appear in the population, indicating a potential copulation activity (Fig. 5b).

### Acknowledgement

The author expresses his thanks to the Belgian Railway Company for providing an inspiring atmosphere for this work, which was not supported by any grant.

### Notes

1. C. Dickens, *Sketches by Boz*: Mudfog and other sketches; Full report of the second meeting of the Mudfog Association

for the Advancement of Everything. London: Chapman and Hall, 1903, pp. 531–50.

2. D. Lodge, *Small World*. Penguin Books, 1985 (Prologue).

3. Azo Koh, The chemical and biological implications, applications and complications of zippery mechanisms. *JIR* **3** (1956), 9–15.

4. B. J. Rubin, If you snip, don't zip! *New Engl. J. Med.*, **315** (1986), 1234.

5. O. Novick, The solution of the Israeli water problem. *JIR*, 15 (1966), 4.

6. L. Ehrenberg and G. Von Ehrenstein, Gonad temperature and spontaneous mutation rate in man. *Nature*, **180** (1957), 1433.

7. L. Mounthard, Considerations of some aspects of the conditions to be fulfilled to reduce the mutation risk in male humans by adequate clothing modifications. *JIR*, **6** (1958), 16–17.

8. R. G. Vines, Evaporation control: a method of treating large water storages. In V. K. LaMer (ed.), *Retardation of evaporation by monolayers*, pp. 137–60. Academic Press, 1962.

9. G. Stanhill, A new method of reducing evaporation. *JIR*, **18** (2) (1970), 56–7.

10. R. F. Howmiller, A comment on Stanhill's evaporation reduction method – possible effects upon water quality. *JIR*, **21** (2) (1975), 11.

11. J. M. Williams, Breast cancer induced by overdose of water. *JIR*, **18** (3) (1971), 85–6.

12. N. L. Caroline and H. Schwartz, Chicken soup rebound and relapse of pneumonia. *Chest*, **67** (2) (1975), 215.

13. K. Saletkhoo, A. Januszkiewicz and M. A. Sackner, Effect of drinking hot water, cold water and chicken soup on nasal mucus velocity and nasal airflow resistance. *Chest*, **74** (1982), 408.

14. S. Idso, Speculation anticipates discovery. *Speculations in Science and Technology*, **10** (1987), 81.

15. P. Thomas and P. J. Gurash, Dust devils on Mars. *Science*, **230** (1986), 175.

16. X. Peery Mental, NO–acetol. *JIR*, **13** (1965), 62.

17. H. S. Wolff, The house cricket as a temperature sensor. *JIR*, **18** (1) (1969), 17–21.

18. S. A. Rudin, The psychoanalysis of US missile failures. *JIR*, **10** (1961), 13–14.
19. J. L. de Lucas, Definition of a dark bulb. In G. H. Scher (ed.), *The Best of JIR*. pp. 180–1. Workman Publ. Co., 1983.
20. M. Conrad, Synthesis of diisopropyl fluorophosphate from Colgate toothpaste. *JIR*, **23** (3) (1977), 26.
21. J. C. Holden, Fake tectonics and continental drip. *JIR*, **22** (2) (1976), 26–7.
22. J. Schmidtke and M. Krawczak, A stable dimorphism in the common paper clip (*Clipus papyrus* Comm). *JIR*, **32** (3) (1987), 2–4.

# Index